GIG BAG SERIES

FOR BASSISTS

BASS
SCALES

EXCLUSIVELY DISTRIBUTED BY

HAL•LEONARD®

Cover design: Fresh Lemon
Project editor: Ed Lozano
Compiled and edited by Joe Dineen
Music engraving by Mark Bridges

This book Copyright © 1997 by Amsco Publications,
A Division of Music Sales Corporation, New York

Order No. AM 942084
ISBN-13: 978-0-8256-3695-0

Contents

Contents

Contents

Introduction

This book is a reference guide for bassists. It is not intended as a method book, but rather as a reference book of scales that are easily accessible to the beginner or advanced bassist. Regardless of your musical interest, this book contains the majority of scales you will encounter in most styles of music (rock, jazz, country, or blues). Strong scale knowledge will help build familiarity with the fretboard and help develop technical ability.

The fifteen scales covered in this book are:
• major (Ionian)
• natural minor (Aeolian)
• Dorian
• Phrygian
• Lydian
• Mixolydian
• Locrian
• harmonic minor
• jazz melodic minor
• Lydian flat-seven
• whole tone
• diminished (whole-half)
• pentatonic (major)
• pentatonic (minor)
• blues scale (with major third and flatted fifth)
Although there are many more scales available, these scales types were chosen for their popularity as well as their usefulness.

The Gig Bag Book of Bass Scales has been designed with the player in mind. You don't have to go to your bookshelf to find that bulky chord encyclopedia that your music stand can't even hold up, you don't have to break the spine of the book to get it to stay open, and it doesn't take up all the space on your music stand. It is easy-to-carry and easy-to-use. We hope that this book will serve as a valuable reference source during your years as a developing bassist.

How to Use this Book

It is strongly recommended that you develop a practice regimen in which you devote some time to scale study. If you practice one hour each session, then devote fifteen or twenty minutes to scale study. Another approach would be to practice your warm-up exercises with a different scale each day.

Here are some helpful tips:

- At the top of each page you will find the scale type and to the right you'll find the scale formula (W = whole-step and H = half-step).
- Notice that there are five suggested scale types along with their fingerings. (The scale types and fingerings are only suggested guidelines; you are encouraged to develop your own scale types and fingerings.)
- The scales are written in both standard notation and *tablature*. You will find a fretboard diagram at the bottom of the page displaying the scale pattern (the root of the scale appears as a circle while the other scale tones appear as black dots).
- In addition, the five fingering types are bracketed at the top of the fretboard diagram to help you visualize the scale pattern all over the neck.

Whether you are looking to develop *chops* (technique) or broaden your scale vocabulary, *The Gig Bag Book of Bass Scales* is for you.

C major (Ionian)

WWHWWWH

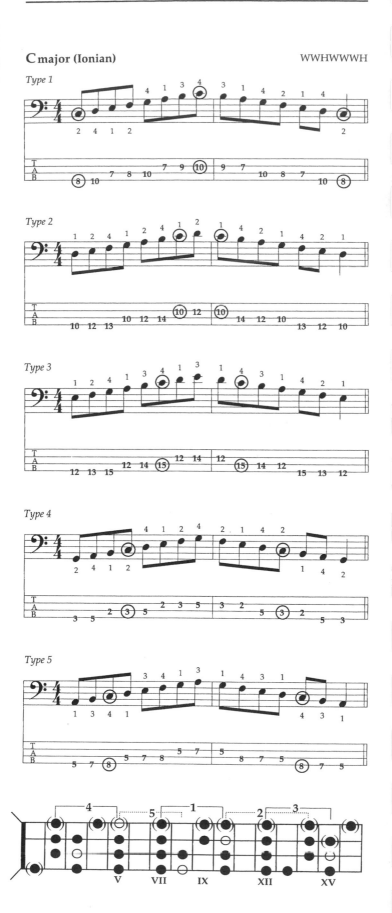

C natural minor (Aeolian)

WHWWHWW

C Dorian

WHWWWHW

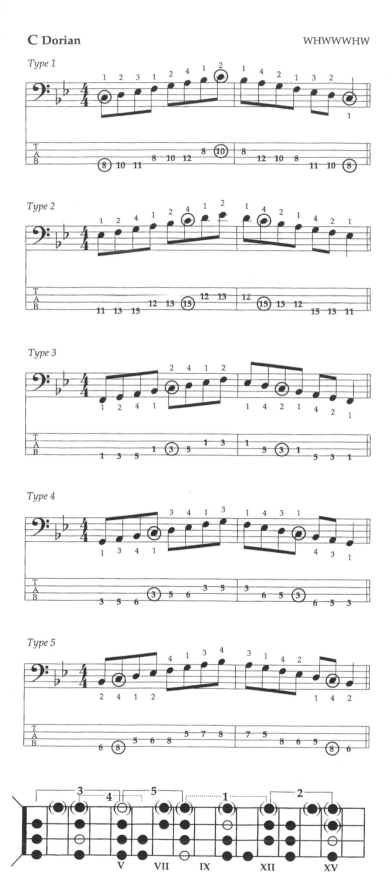

C Phrygian

HWWWHWW

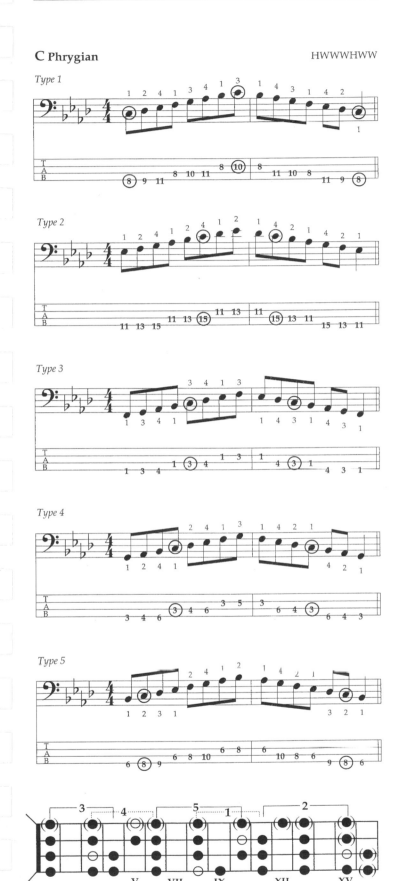

Type 1

Type 2

Type 3

Type 4

Type 5

C Lydian

WWWHWWH

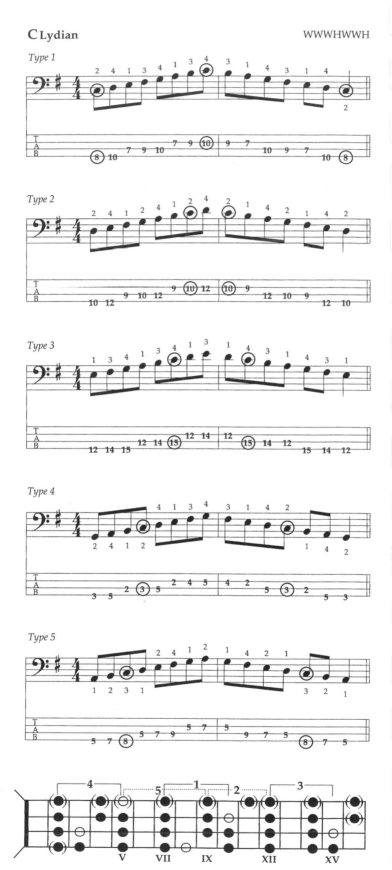

C Mixolydian

WWHWWHW

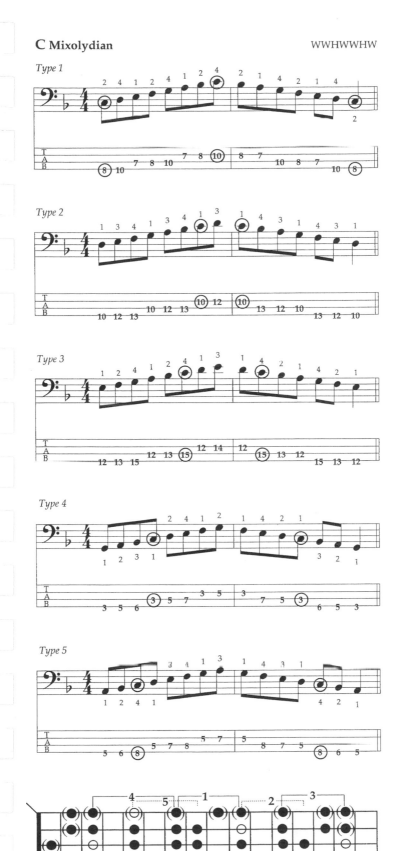

Type 1

Type 2

Type 3

Type 4

Type 5

C Locrian

HWWHWWW

Type 1

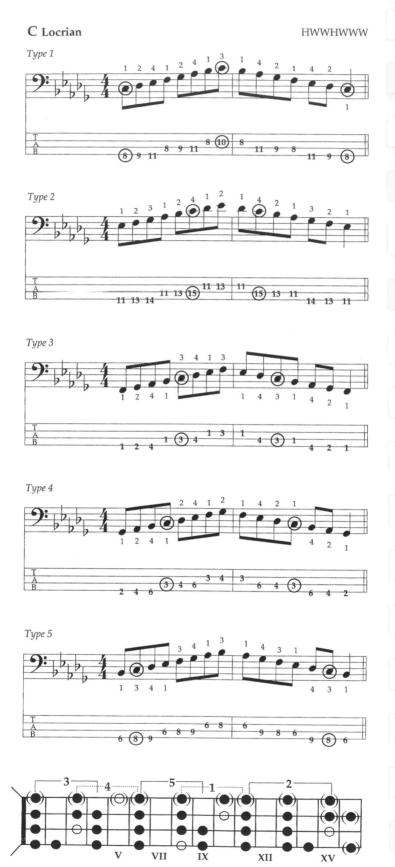

Type 2

Type 3

Type 4

Type 5

C harmonic minor

WHWWHm3H

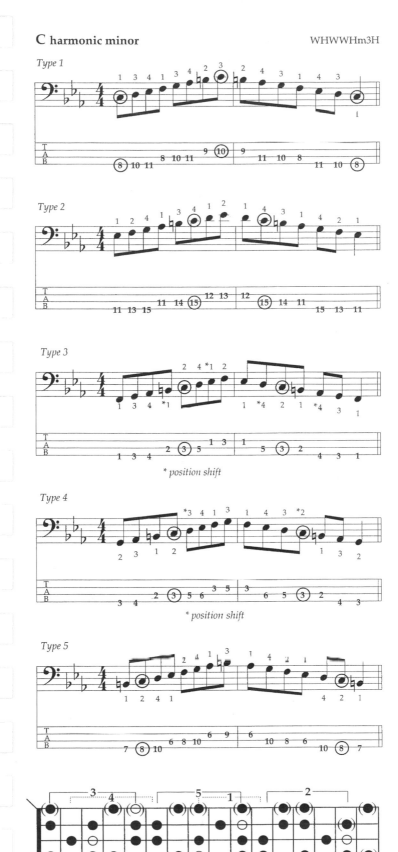

* position shift

* position shift

C jazz melodic minor

WHWWWWH

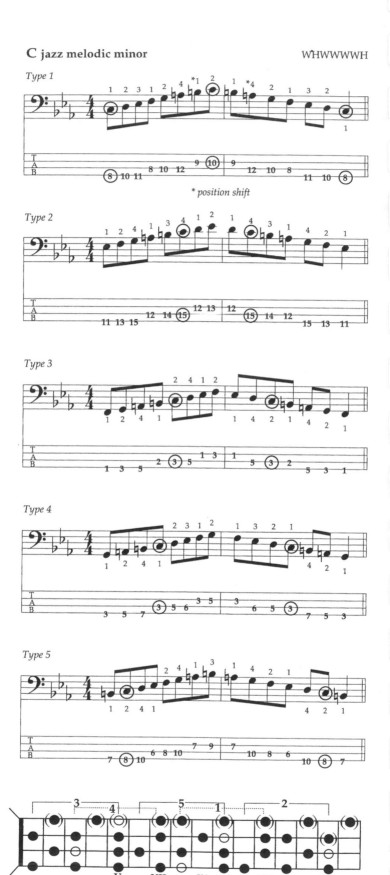

*position shift

C Lydian flat-seven

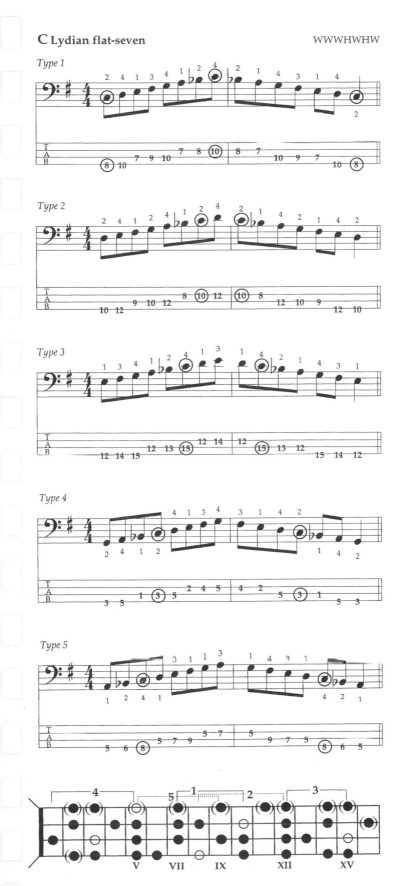

C whole tone

WWWWWW

Type 1

Type 2

C diminished (whole-half)

WHWHWHWH

Type 1

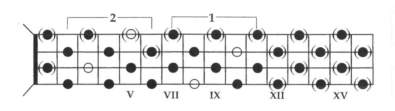

* position shift

Type 2

* position shift

C pentatonic (major)

WWm3Wm3

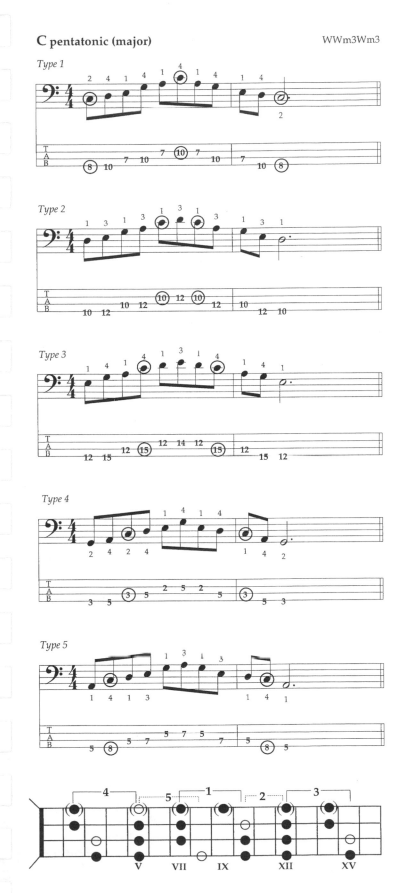

C pentatonic (minor)

m3WWm3W

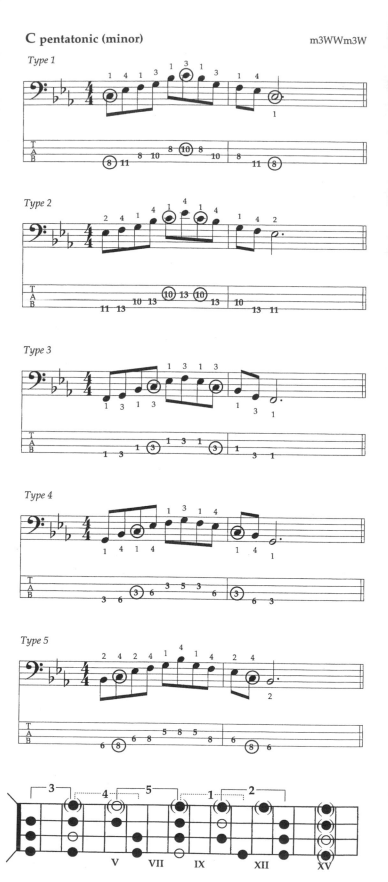

C blues scale (with major third & flatted fifth) m3HHHHm3W

Type 1

* position shift

Type 2

* position shift

Type 3

Type 4

* position shift

Type 5

* position shift

D♭ major (Ionian)

WWHWWWH

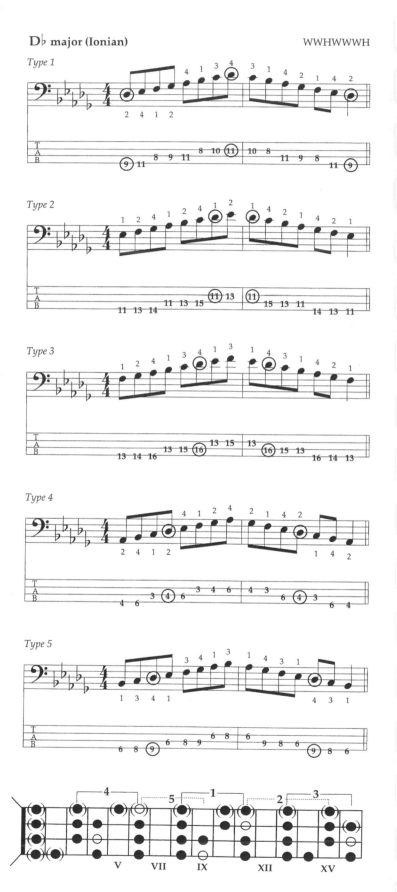

C#/Db natural minor (Aeolian)

WHWWHWW

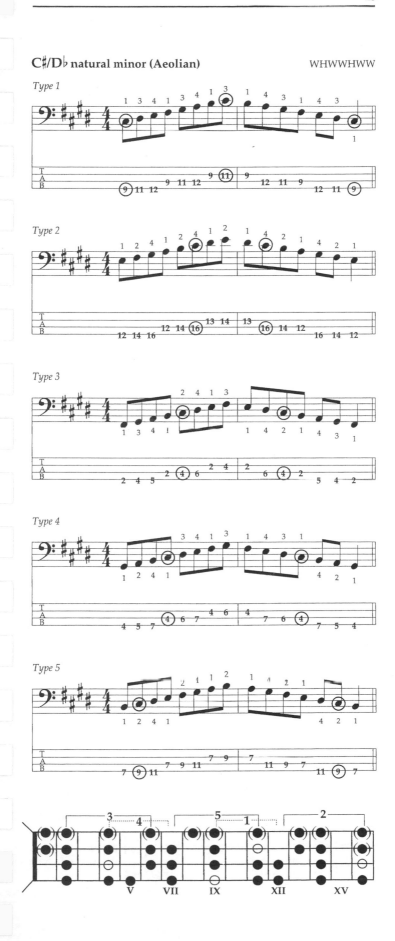

Type 1

Type 2

Type 3

Type 4

Type 5

D♭ Dorian

WHWWWHW

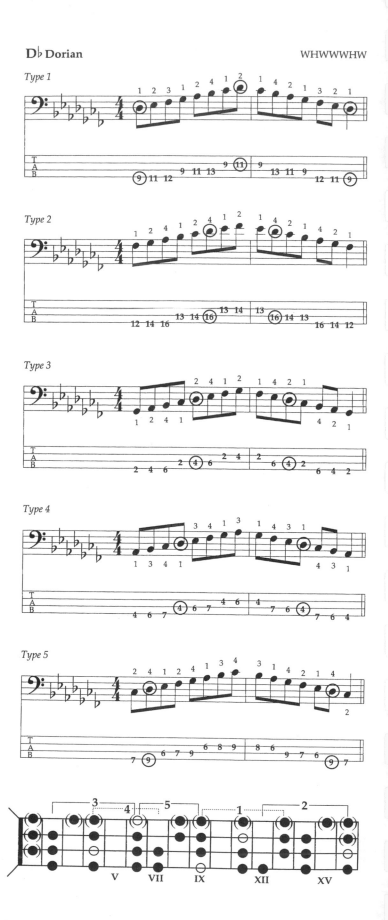

C♯/D♭ Phrygian

HWWWHWW

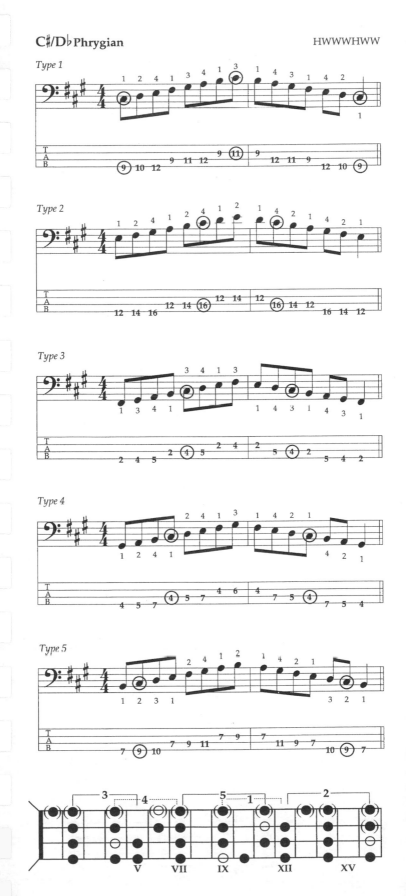

D♭ Lydian WWWHWWH

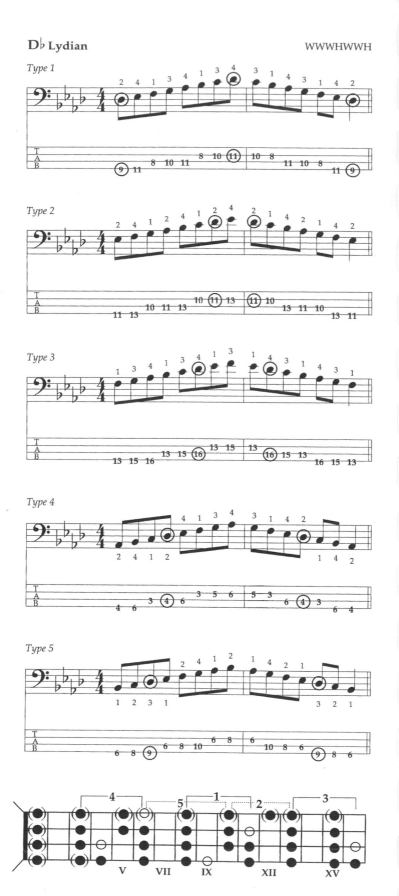

D♭ Mixolydian

WWHWWHW

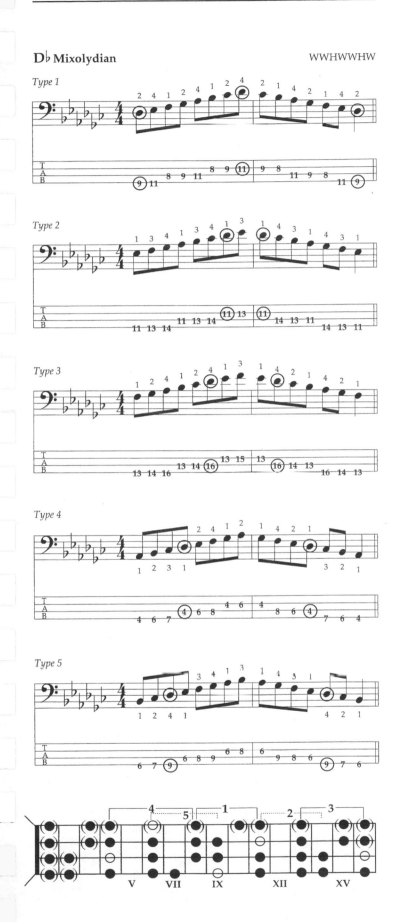

C#/Db Locrian

HWWHWWW

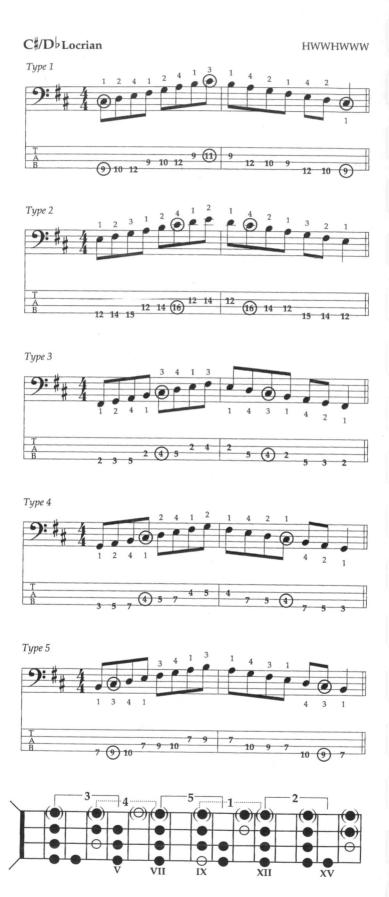

C#/D♭ harmonic minor

WHWWHm3H

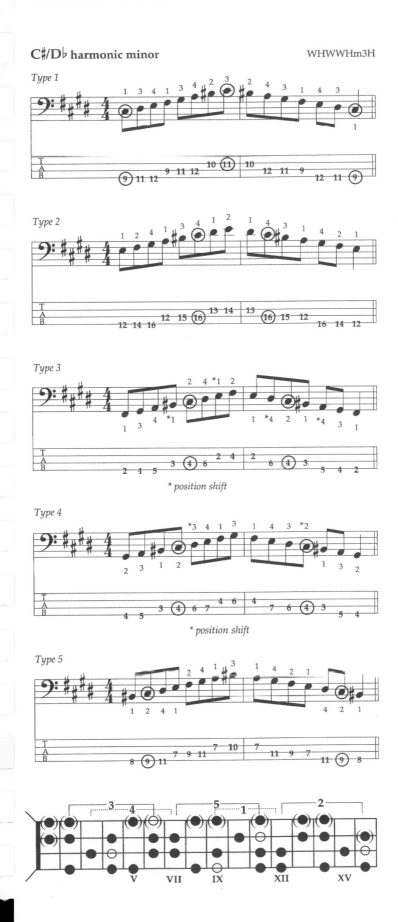

Type 1

Type 2

Type 3

* *position shift*

Type 4

* *position shift*

Type 5

C♯/D♭ jazz melodic minor

WHWWWWH

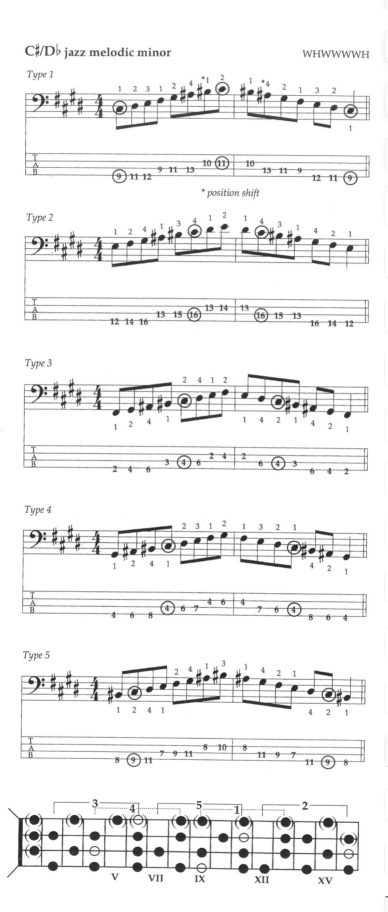

* position shift

D♭ Lydian flat-seven

WWWHWHW

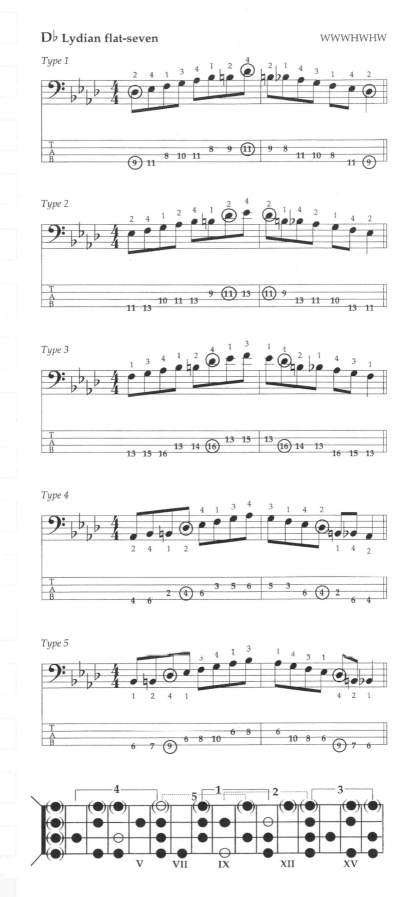

D♭ whole tone

WWWWWW

Type 1

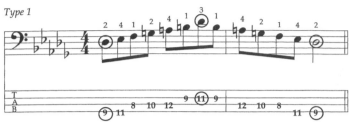

Type 2

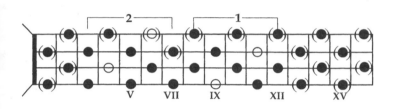

D♭ diminished (whole-half)

WHWHWHWH

Type 1

* *position shift*

Type 2

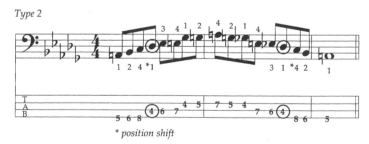

* *position shift*

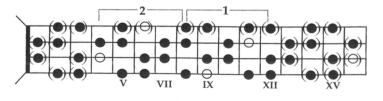

D♭ pentatonic (major)

WWm3Wm3

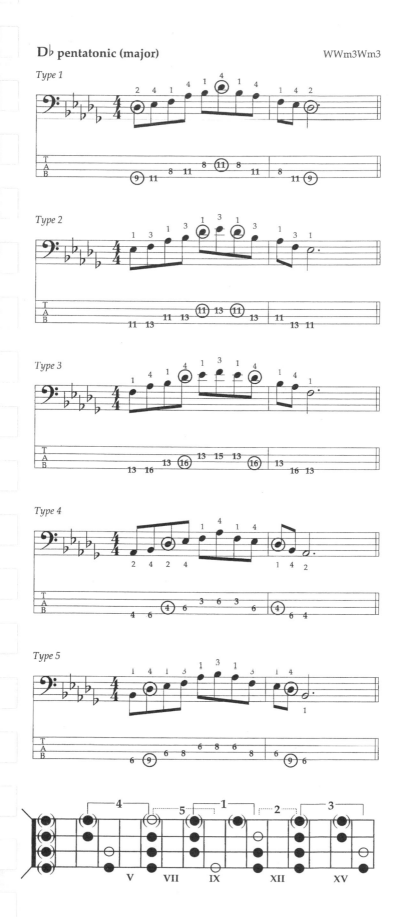

C#/Db pentatonic (minor)

m3WWm3W

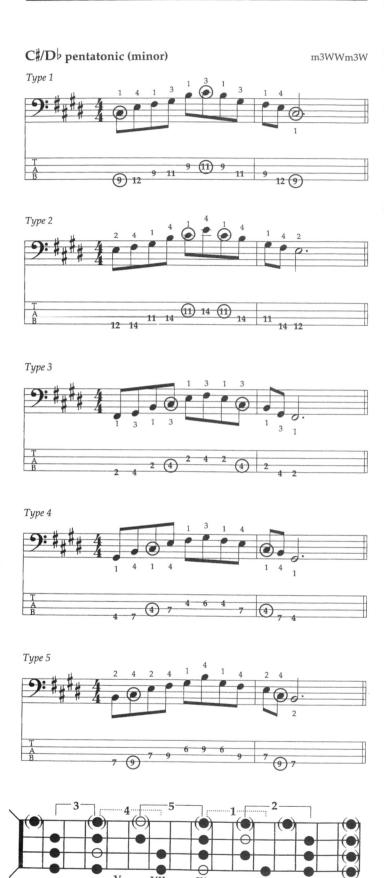

D♭ blues scale (with major third & flatted fifth)   m3HHHHm3W

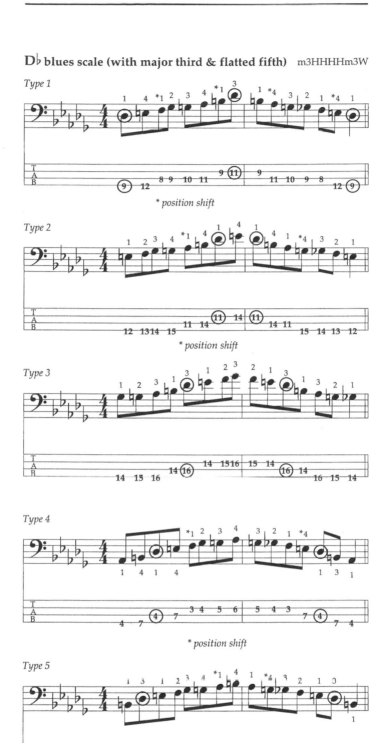

Type 1

* position shift

Type 2

* position shift

Type 3

Type 4

* position shift

Type 5

* position shift

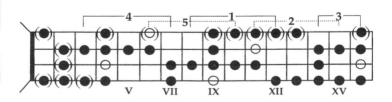

D major (Ionian)

WWHWWWH

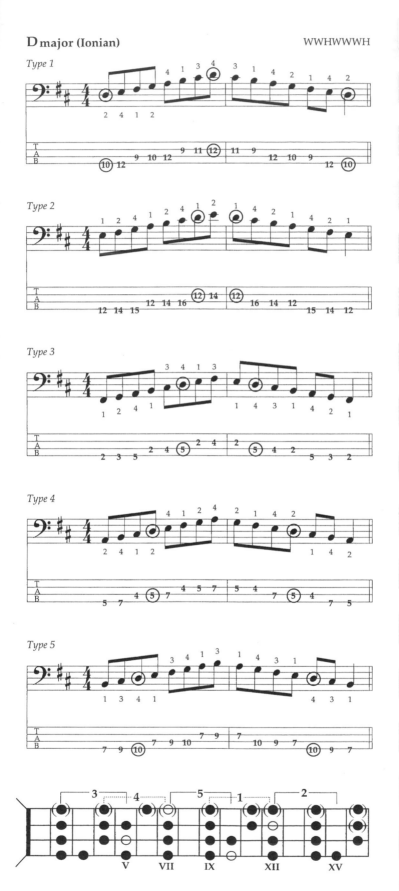

D natural minor (Aeolian)

WHWWHWW

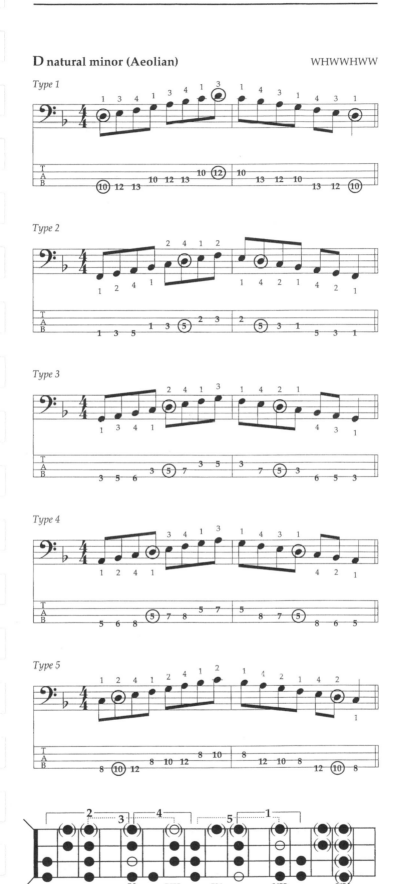

D Dorian

WHWWWHW

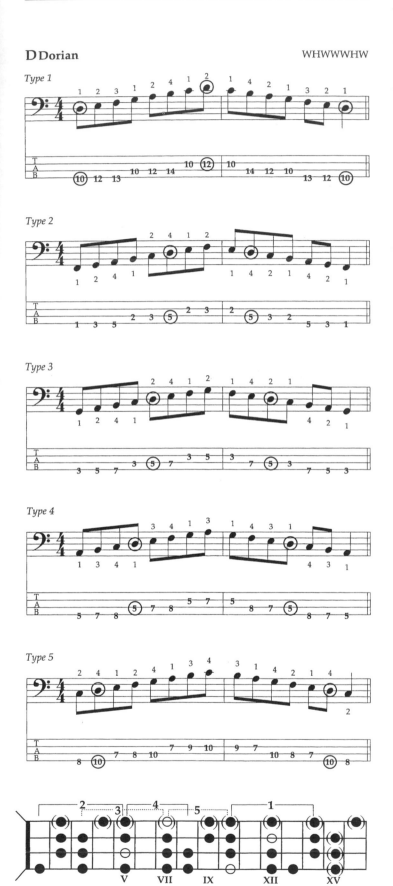

D Phrygian

HWWWHWW

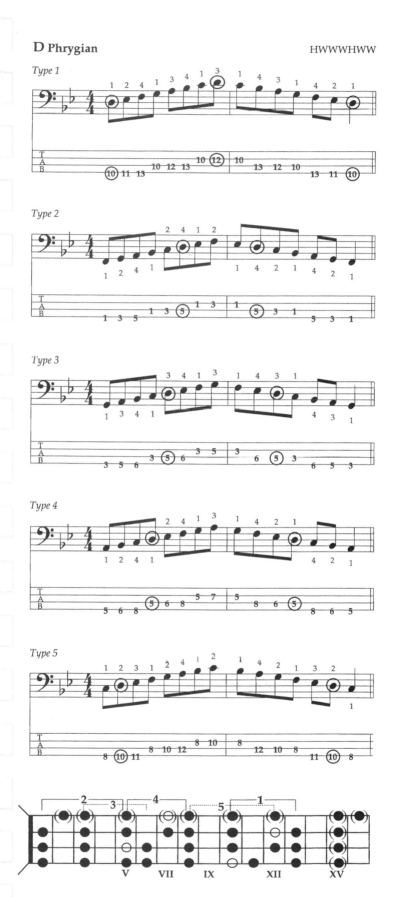

D Lydian

WWWHWWH

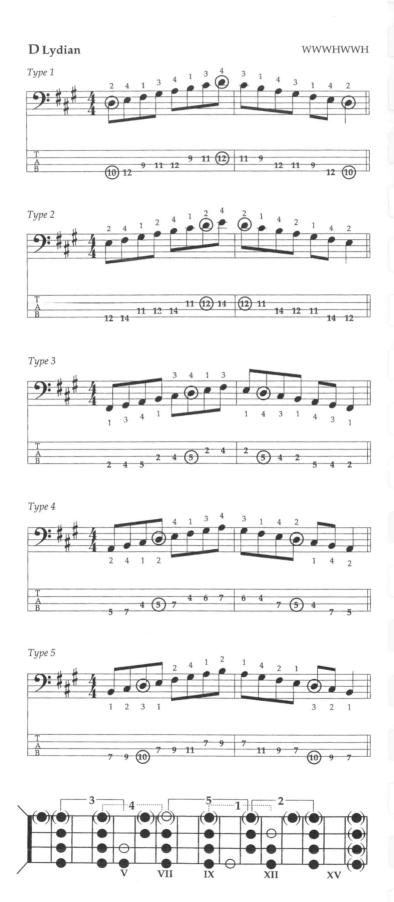

D Mixolydian

WWHWWHW

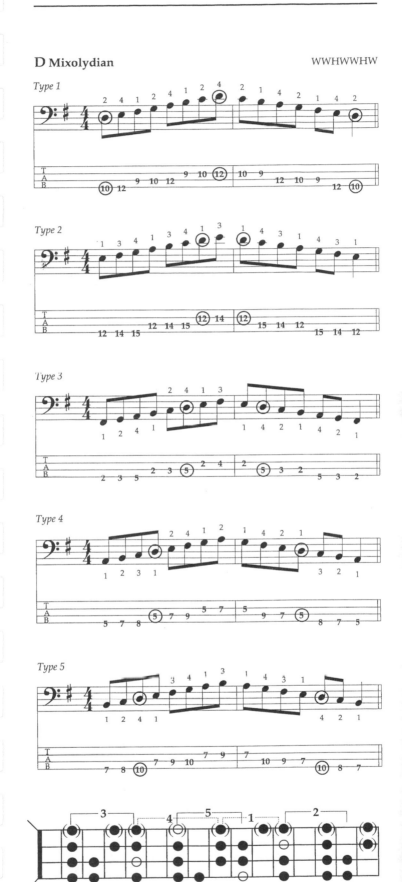

D Locrian

HWWHWWW

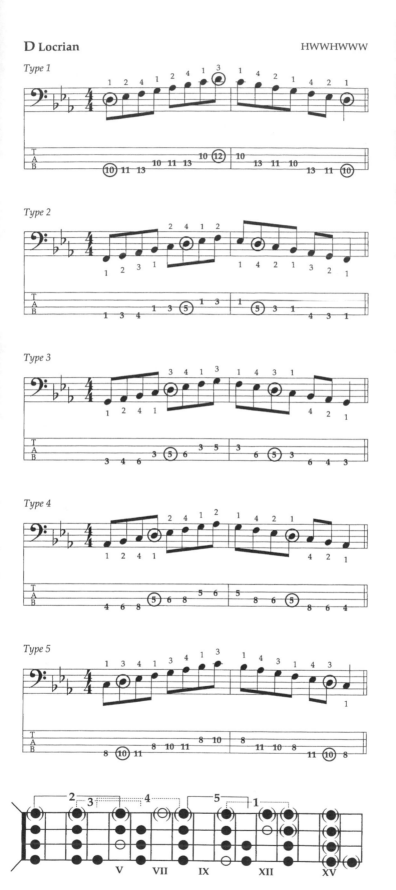

D harmonic minor

WHWWHm3H

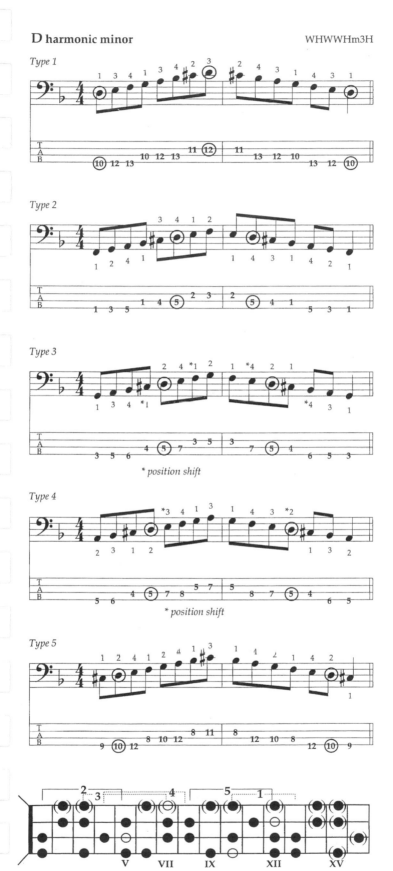

Type 1

Type 2

Type 3

position shift

Type 4

position shift

Type 5

D jazz melodic minor

WHWWWWH

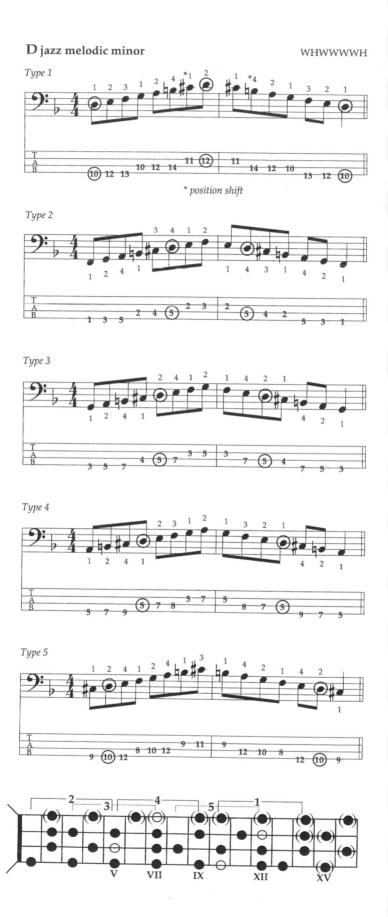

Type 1

* *position shift*

Type 2

Type 3

Type 4

Type 5

D Lydian flat-seven

WWWHWHW

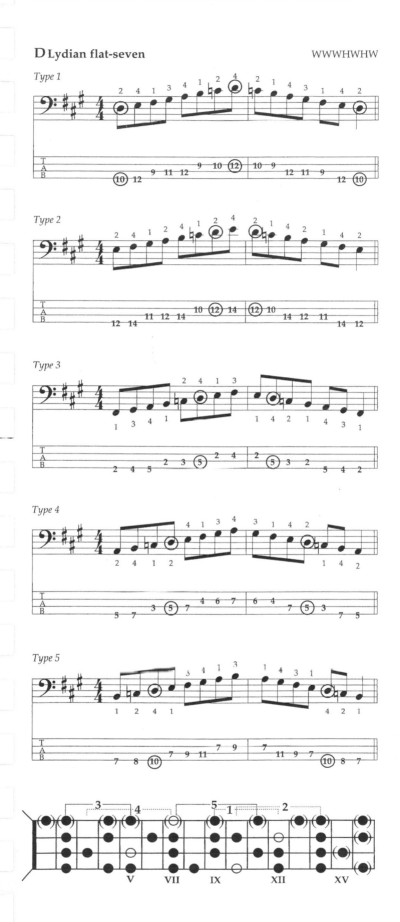

D whole tone

WWWWWW

Type 1

Type 2

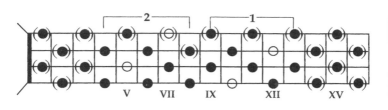

D diminished (whole-half)

WHWHWHWH

Type 1

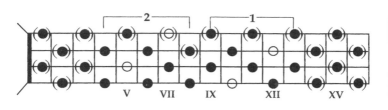

* position shift

Type 2

* position shift

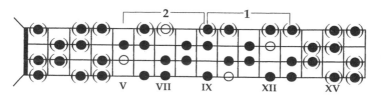

D pentatonic (major)

WWm3Wm3

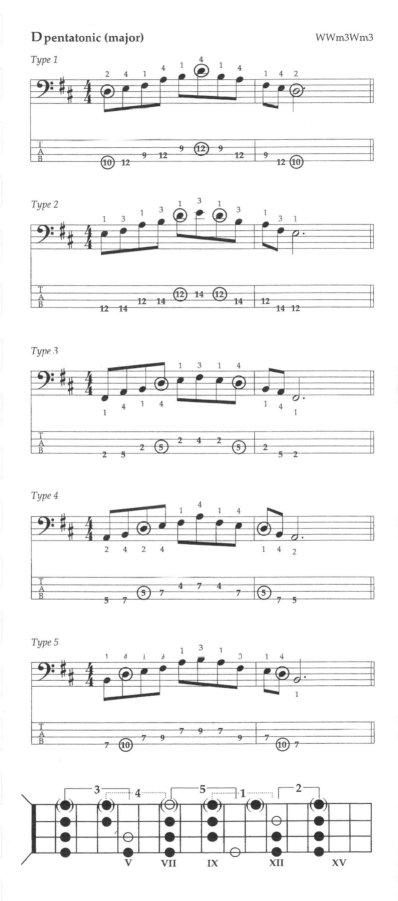

Type 1

Type 2

Type 3

Type 4

Type 5

D pentatonic (minor)

m3WWm3W

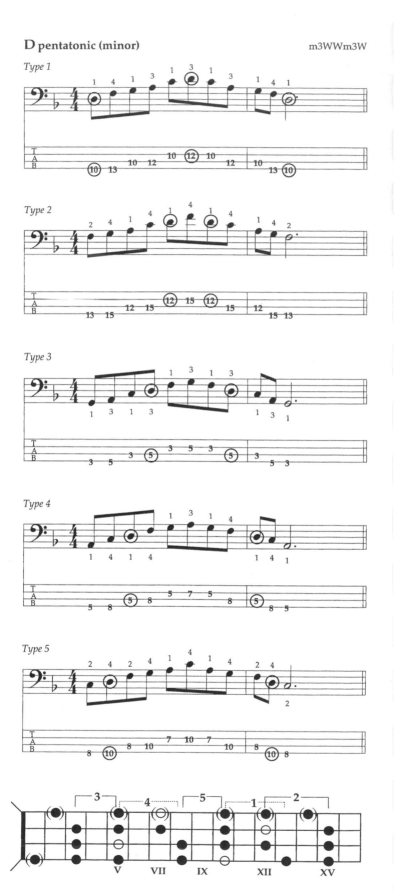

D blues scale (with major third & flatted fifth)   m3HHHHm3W

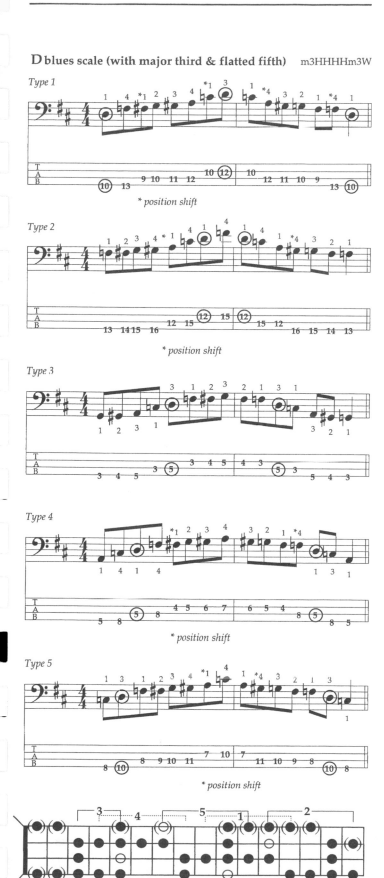

Type 1

position shift

Type 2

position shift

Type 3

Type 4

position shift

Type 5

position shift

E♭ major (Ionian)

WWHWWWH

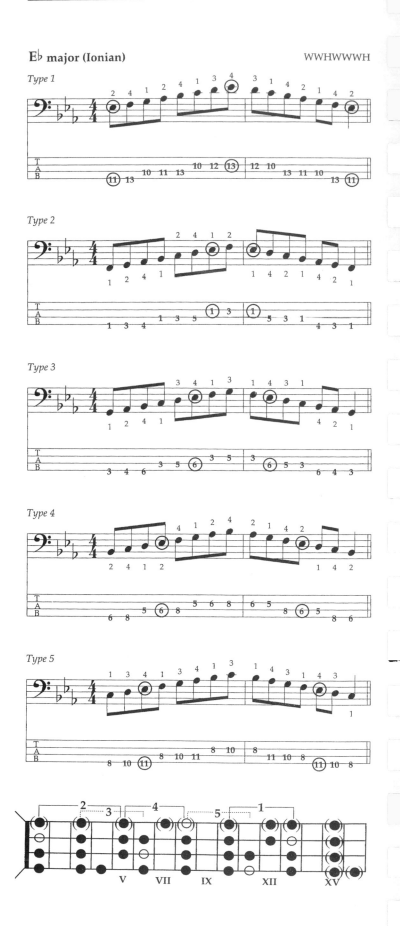

E♭ natural minor (Aeolian)

WHWWHWW

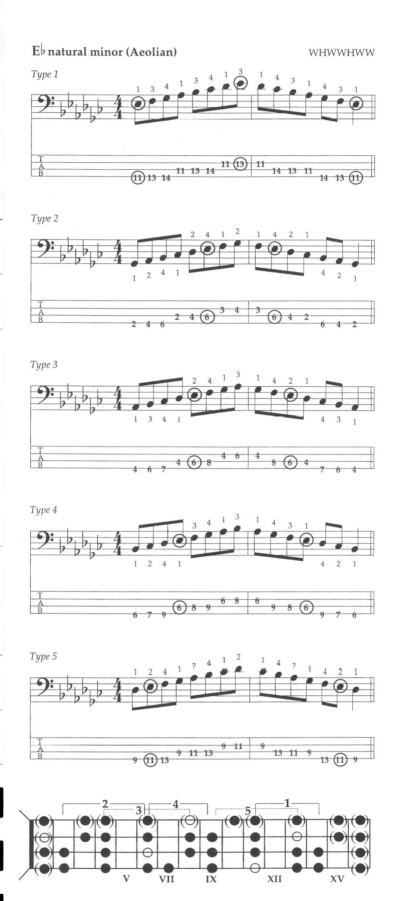

Type 1

Type 2

Type 3

Type 4

Type 5

E♭ Dorian

WHWWWHW

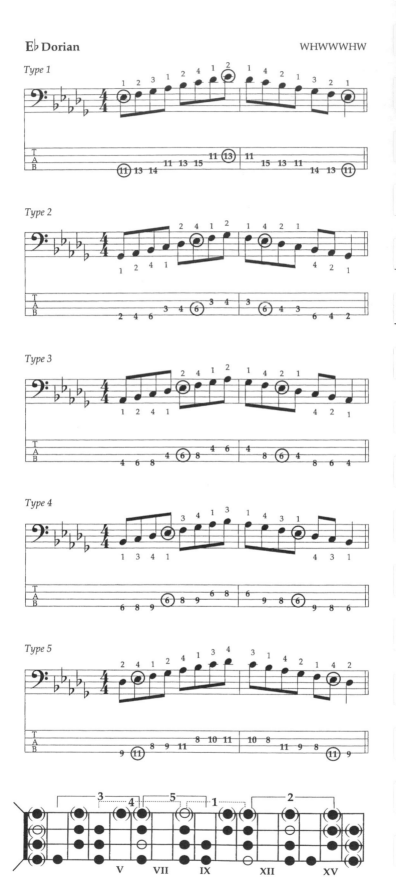

Eb Phrygian

HWWWHWW

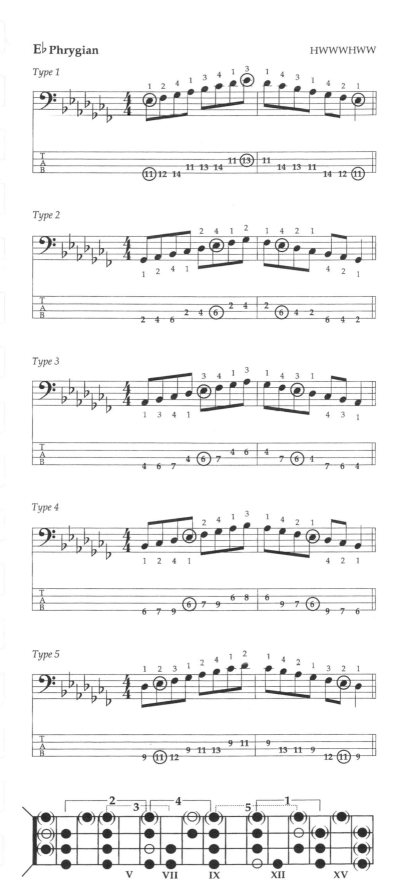

E♭ Lydian

WWWHWWH

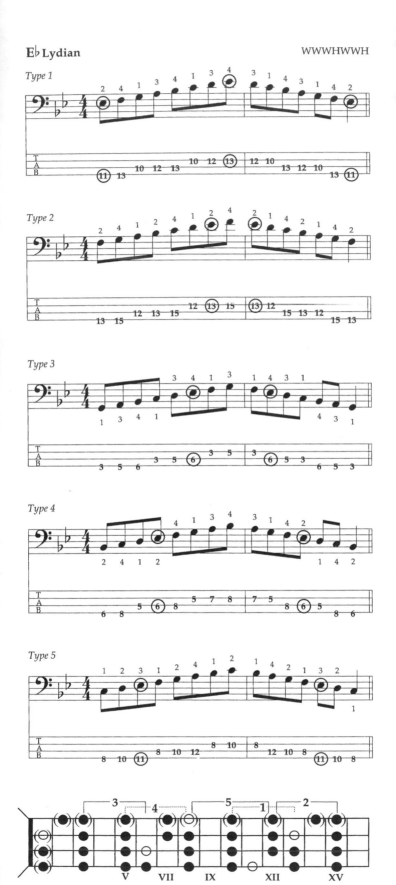

E♭ Mixolydian

WWHWWHW

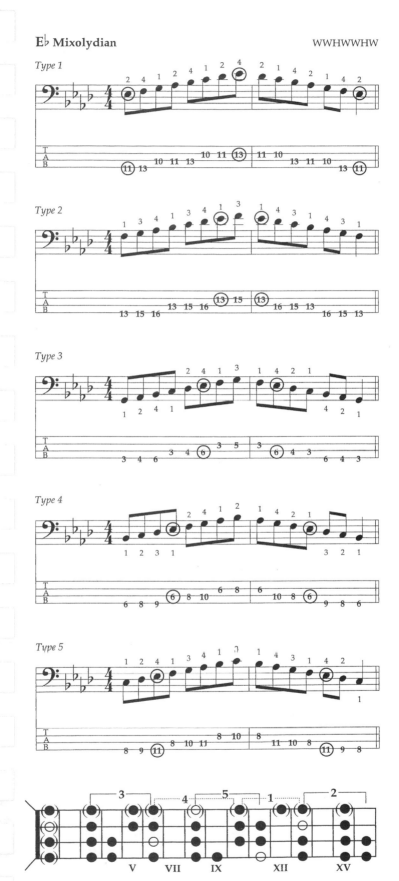

D#/Eb Locrian

HWWHWWW

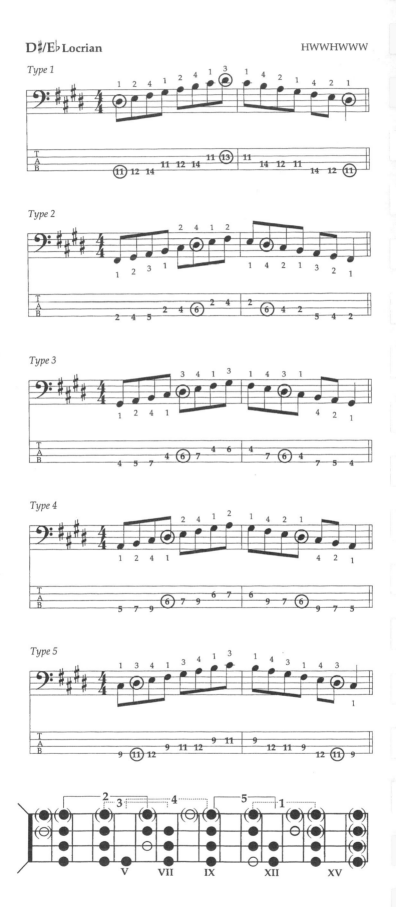

E♭ harmonic minor

WHWWHm3H

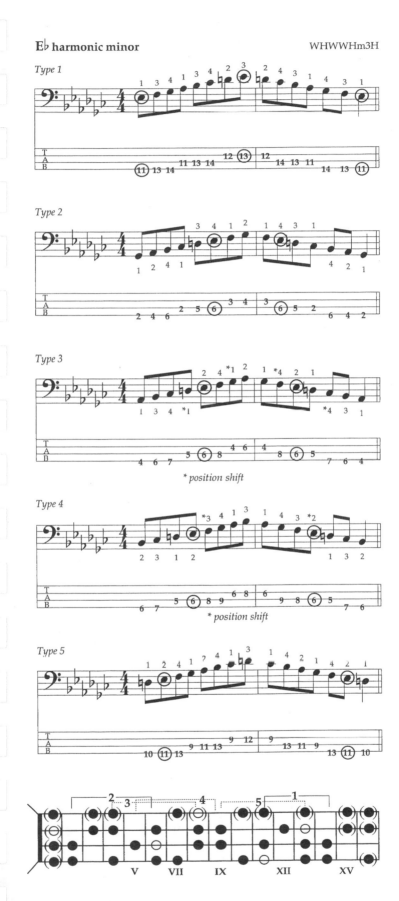

Type 1

Type 2

Type 3

* position shift

Type 4

* position shift

Type 5

E♭ jazz melodic minor

WHWWWWH

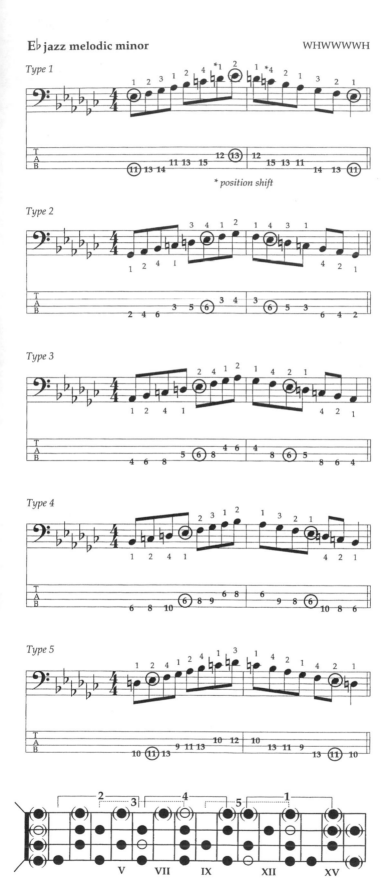

Type 1

* position shift

Type 2

Type 3

Type 4

Type 5

E♭ Lydian flat-seven

WWWHWHW

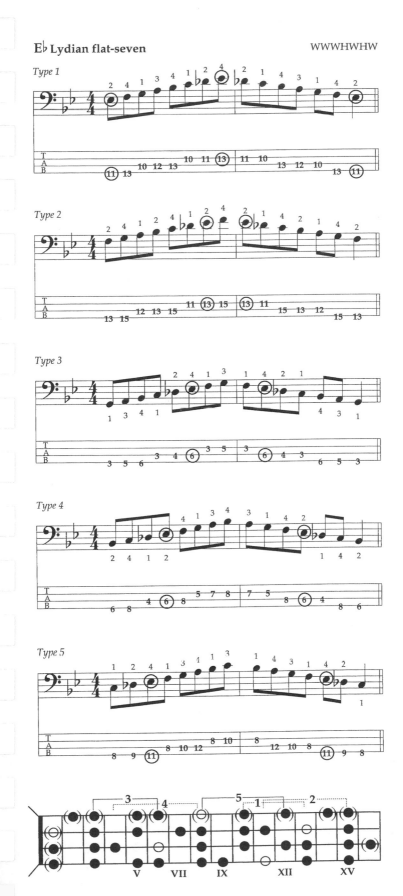

E♭ whole tone
WWWWWW

Type 1

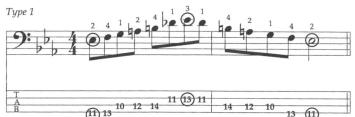

Type 2

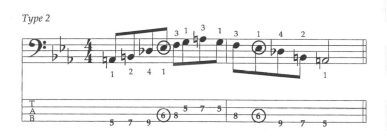

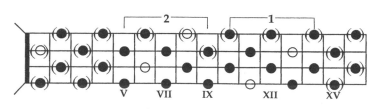

E♭ diminished (whole-half)
WHWHWHWH

Type 1

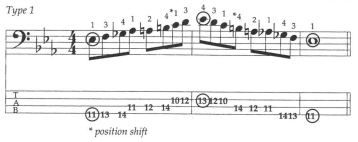

* *position shift*

Type 2

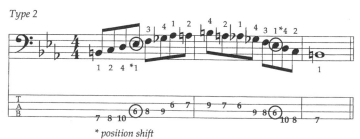

* *position shift*

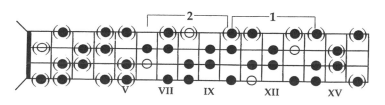

E♭ pentatonic (major)

WWm3Wm3

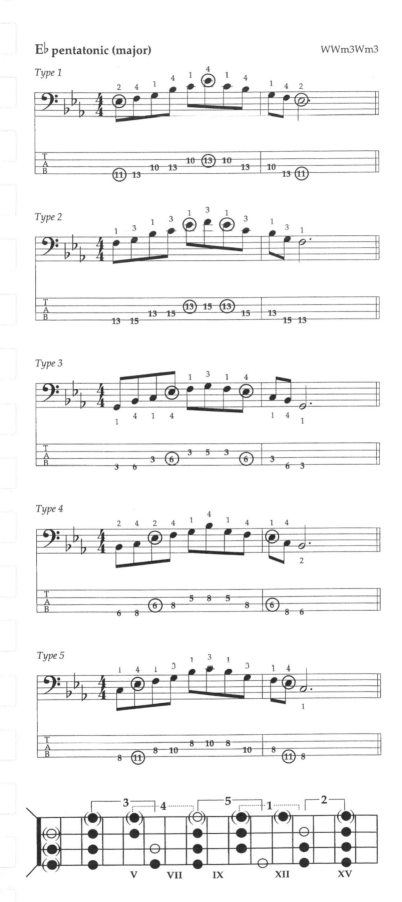

E♭ pentatonic (minor)

m3WWm3W

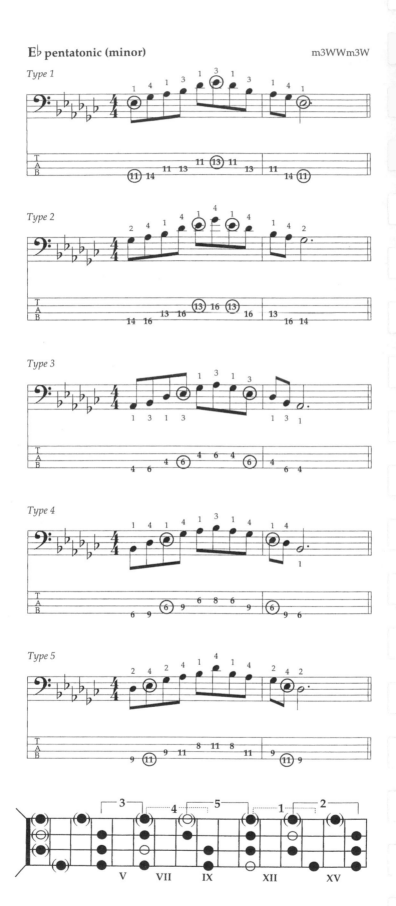

E♭ blues scale (with major third & flatted fifth)   m3HHHHm3W

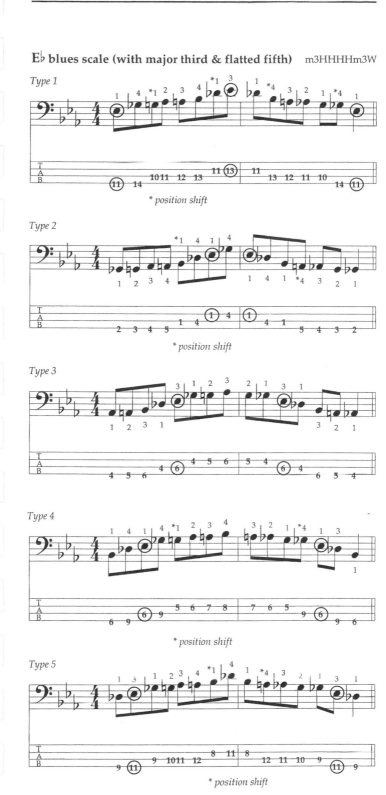

Type 1

* position shift

Type 2

* position shift

Type 3

Type 4

* position shift

Type 5

* position shift

E major (Ionian)

WWHWWWH

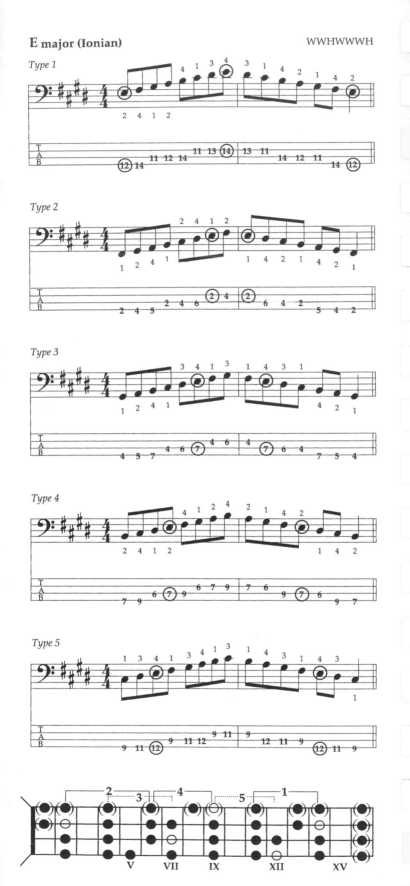

E natural minor (Aeolian)

WHWWHWW

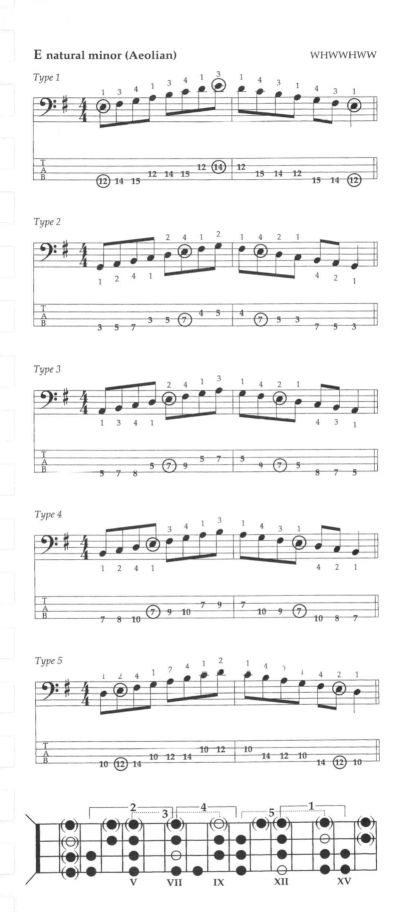

E Dorian

WHWWWHW

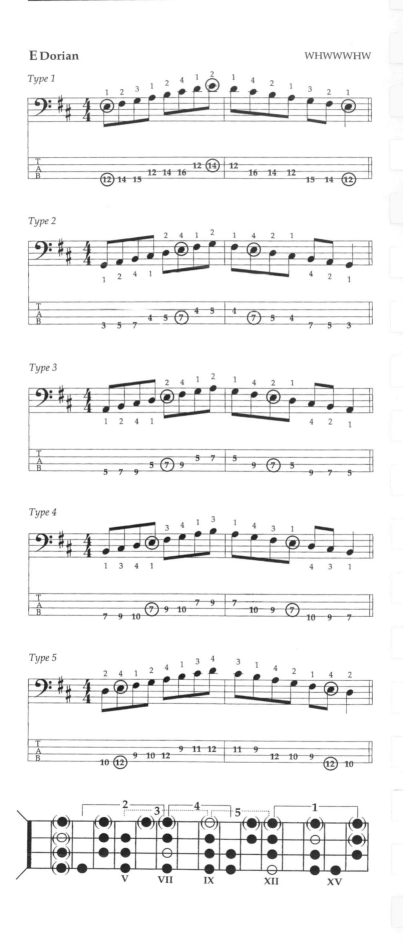

E Phrygian

HWWWHWW

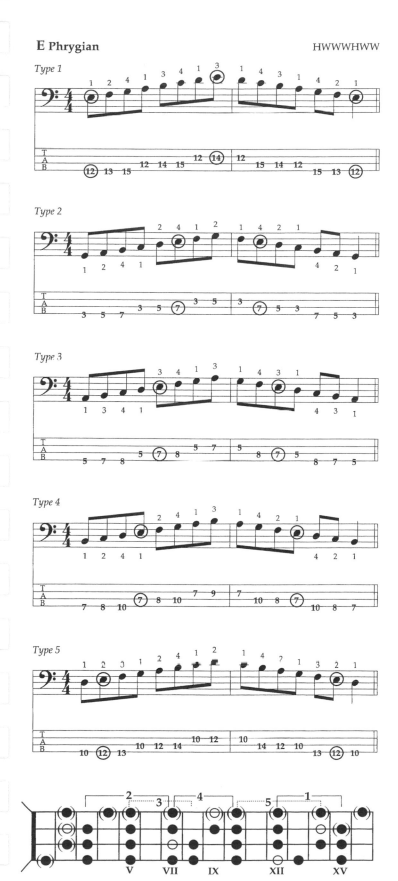

E Lydian

WWWHWWH

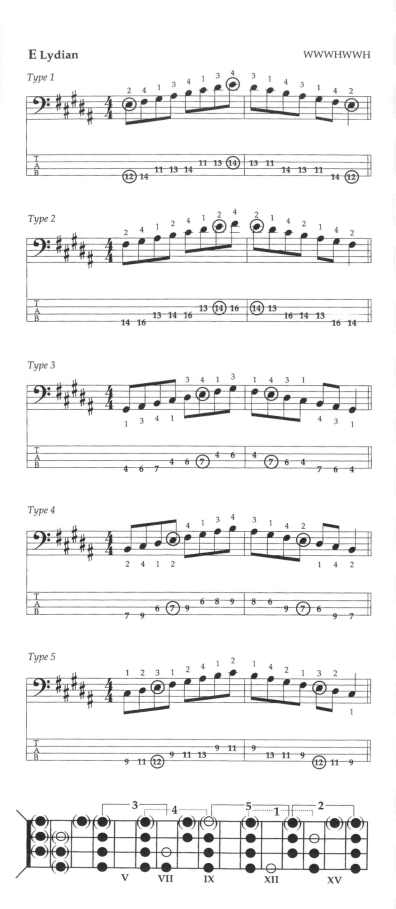

E Mixolydian

WWHWWHW

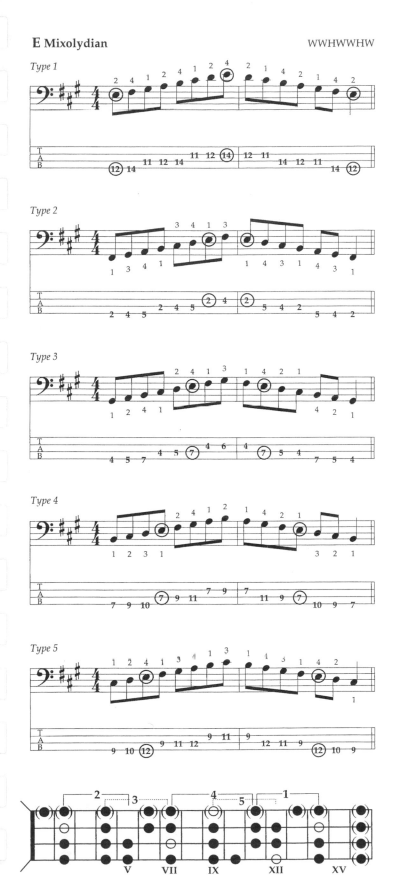

E Locrian

HWWHWWW

Type 1

Type 2

Type 3

Type 4

Type 5

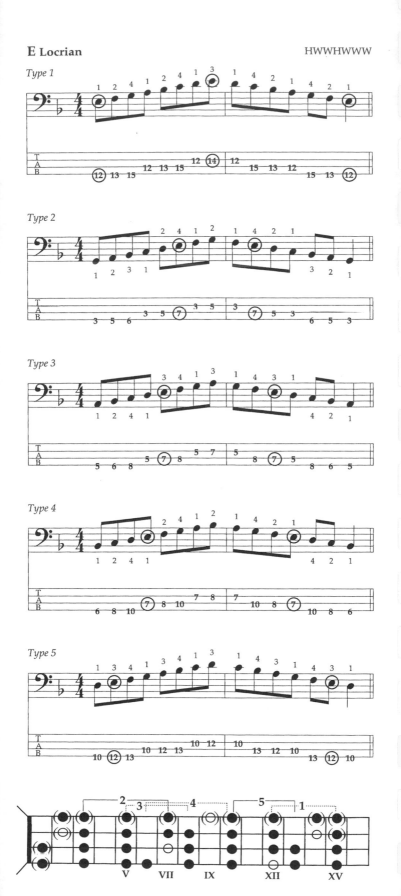

E harmonic minor

WHWWHm3H

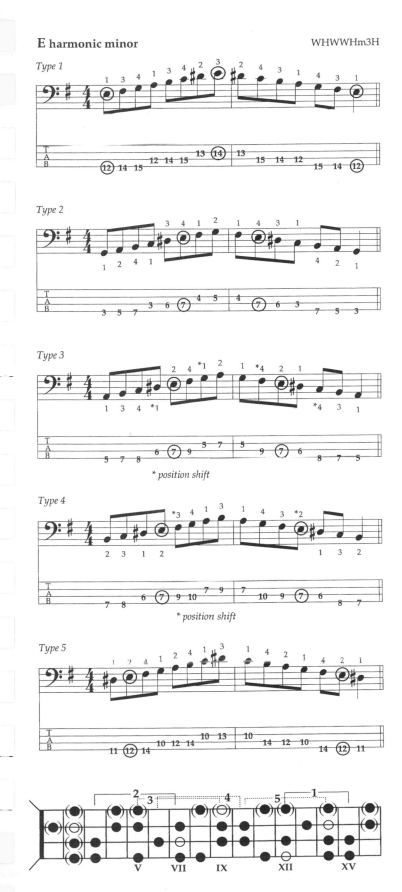

Type 1

Type 2

Type 3

* position shift

Type 4

* position shift

Type 5

E jazz melodic minor

WHWWWWH

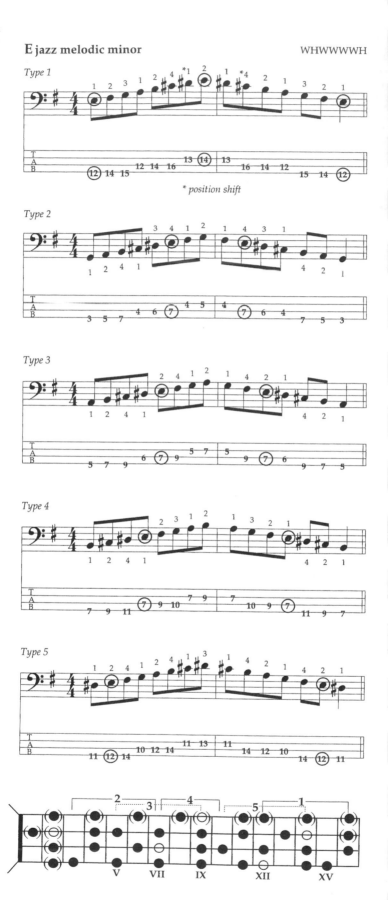

position shift

E Lydian flat-seven

WWWHWHW

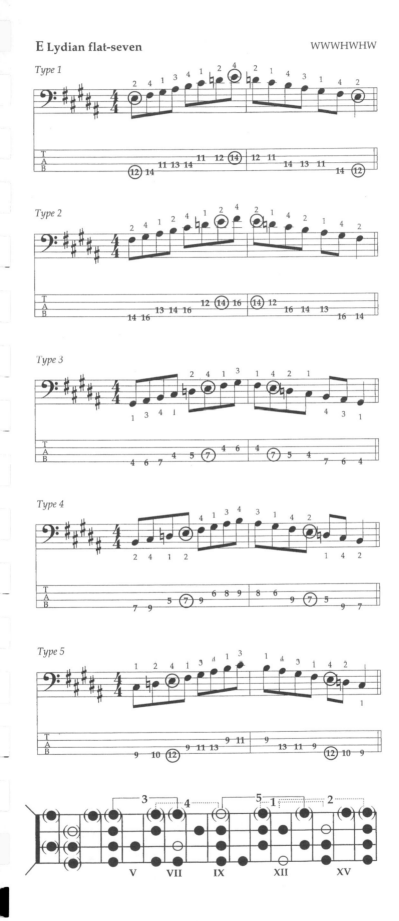

E whole tone

WWWWWW

Type 1

Type 2

E diminished (whole-half)

WHWHWHWH

Type 1

* position shift

Type 2

* position shift

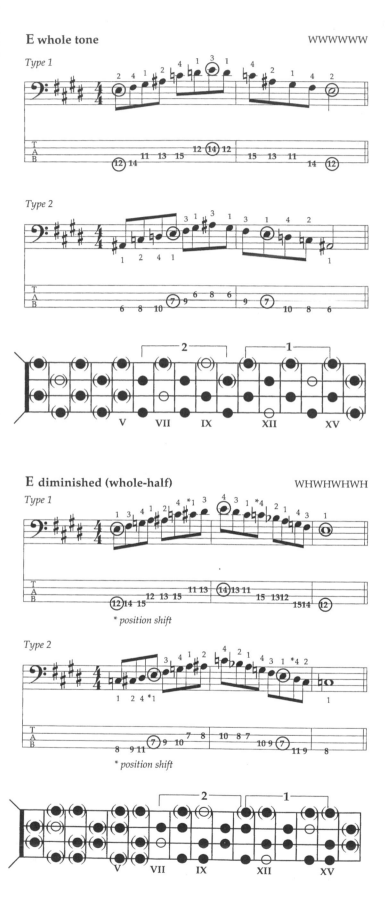

E pentatonic (major)

WWm3Wm3

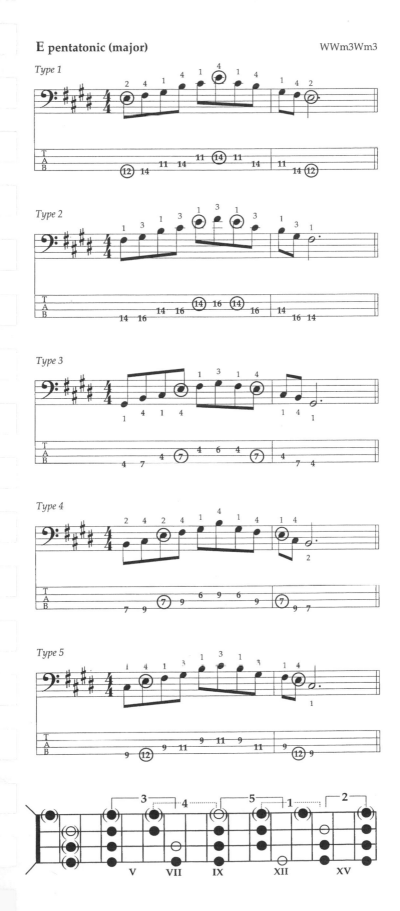

E pentatonic (minor)

m3WWm3W

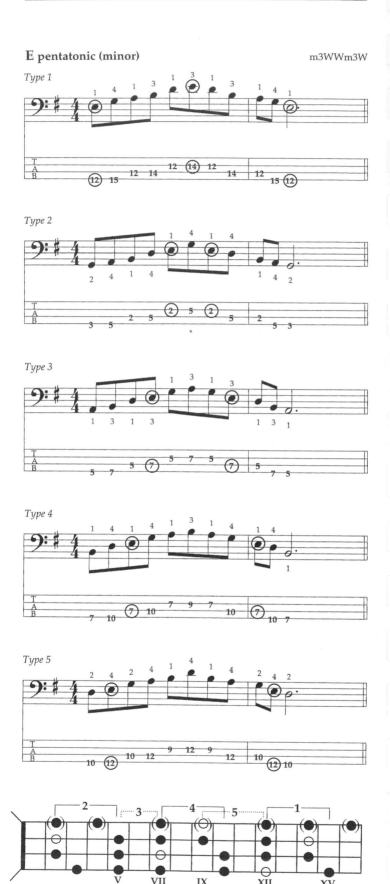

E blues scale (with major third & flatted fifth) m3HHHHm3W

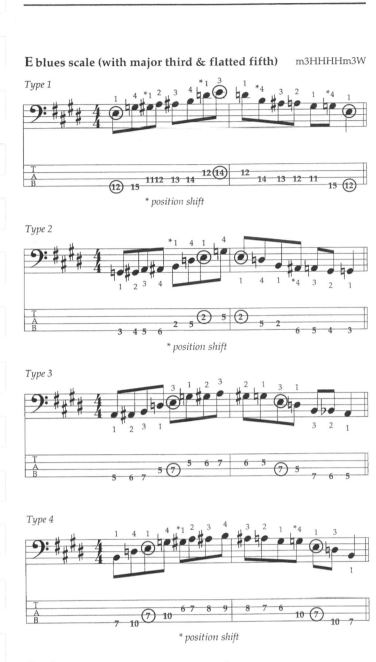

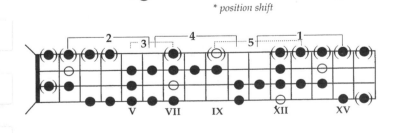

F major (Ionian)

WWHWWWH

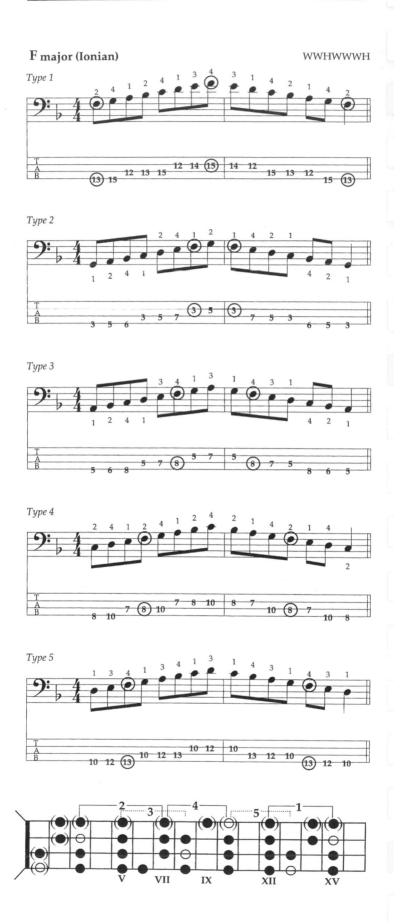

F natural minor (Aeolian)

WHWWHWW

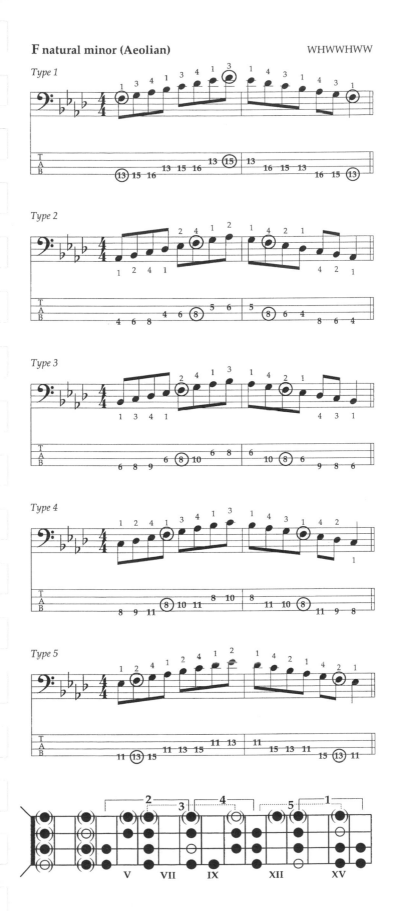

F Dorian

WHWWWHW

Type 1

Type 2

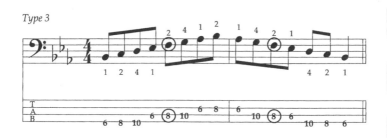

Type 3

Type 4

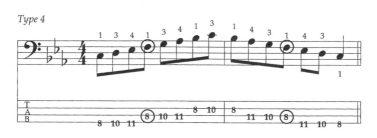

Type 5

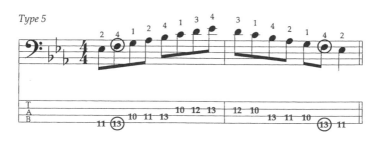

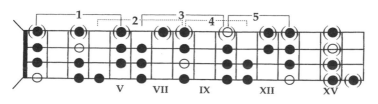

F Phrygian

HWWWHWW

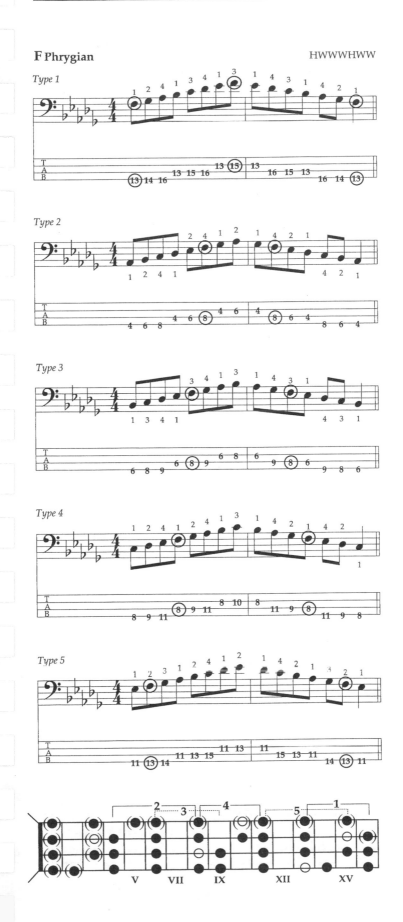

F Lydian

WWWHWWH

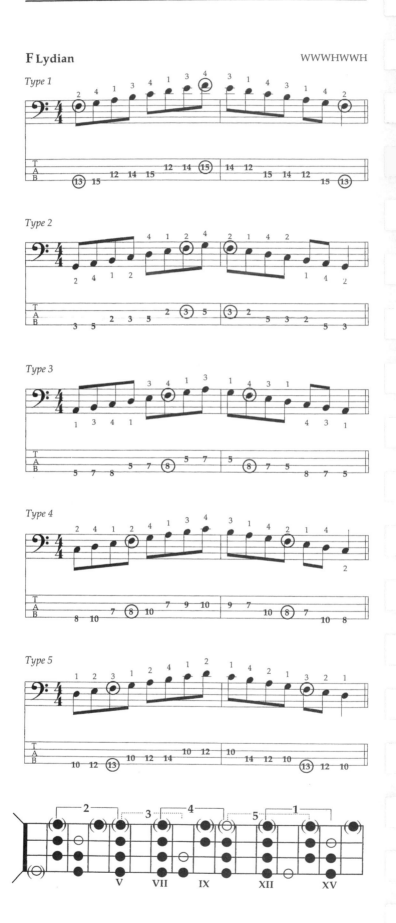

F Mixolydian

WWHWWHW

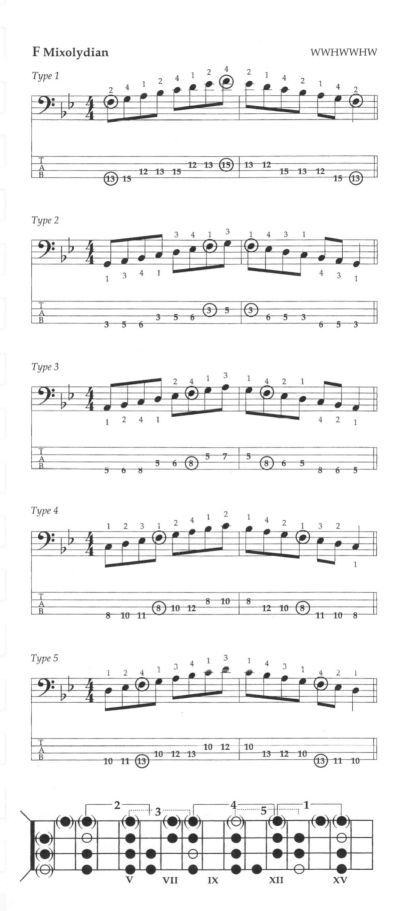

F Locrian

HWWHWWW

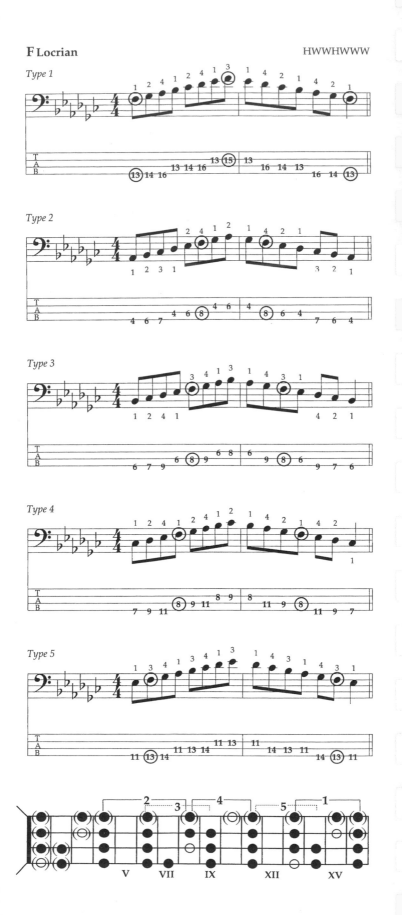

F harmonic minor

WHWWHm3H

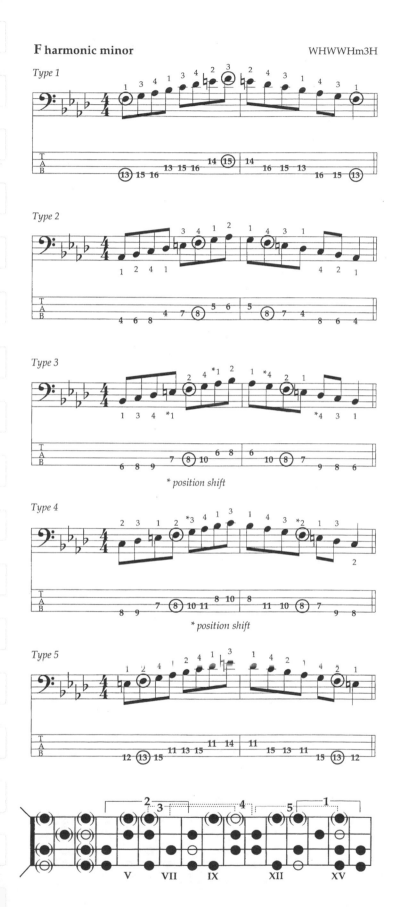

Type 1

Type 2

Type 3

position shift

Type 4

position shift

Type 5

F jazz melodic minor

WHWWWWH

Type 1

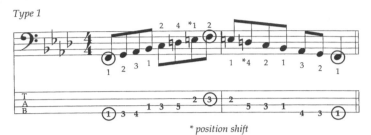

* position shift

Type 2

Type 3

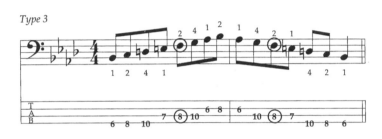

Type 4

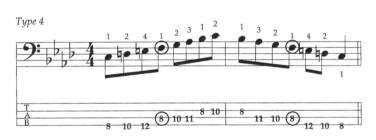

Type 5

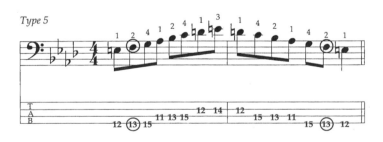

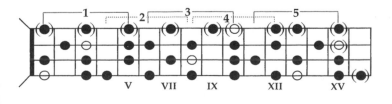

F Lydian flat-seven

WWWHWHW

Type 1

Type 2

Type 3

Type 4

Type 5

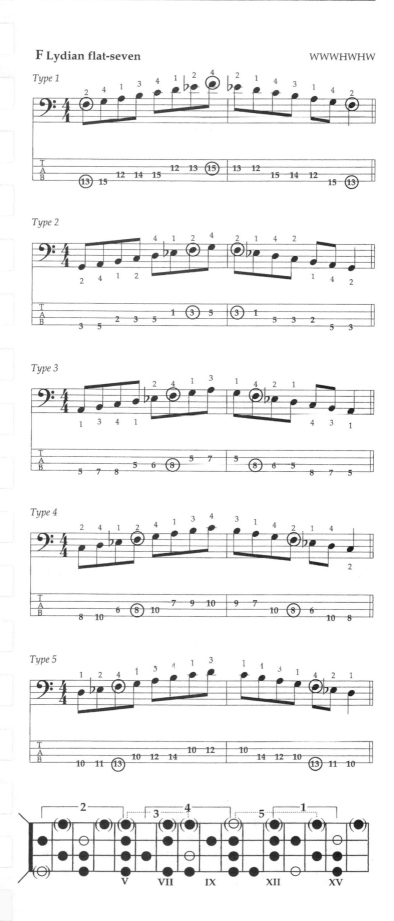

F whole tone

WWWWWW

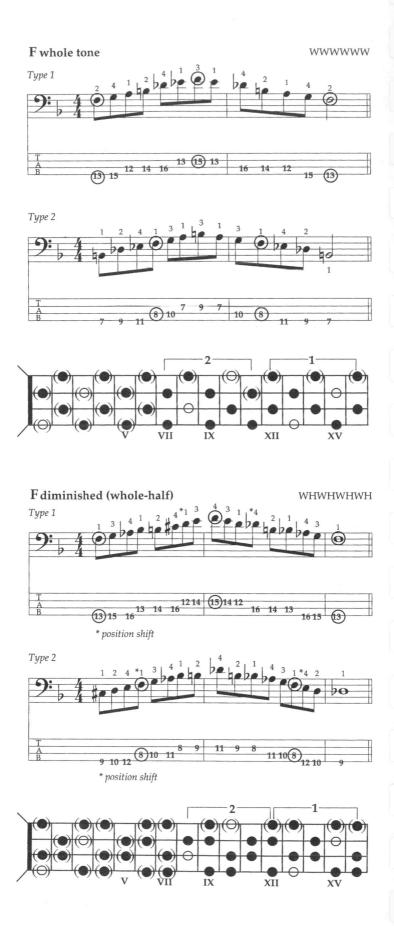

Type 1

Type 2

F diminished (whole-half)

WHWHWHWH

Type 1

* position shift

Type 2

* position shift

F pentatonic (major)

WWm3Wm3

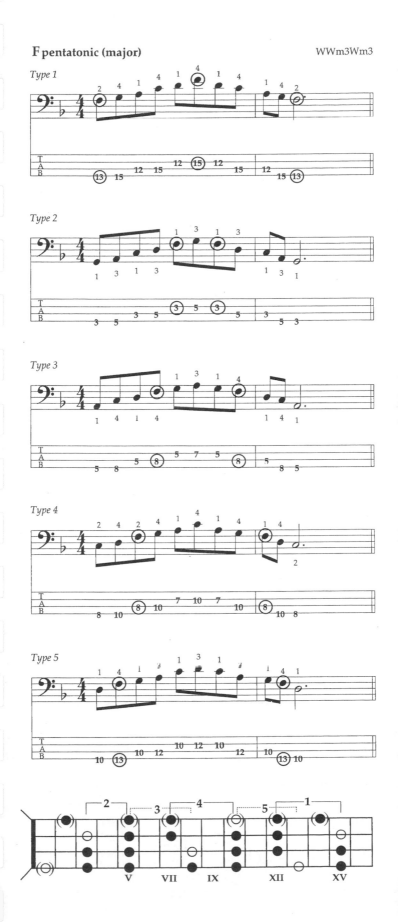

F pentatonic (minor)

m3WWm3W

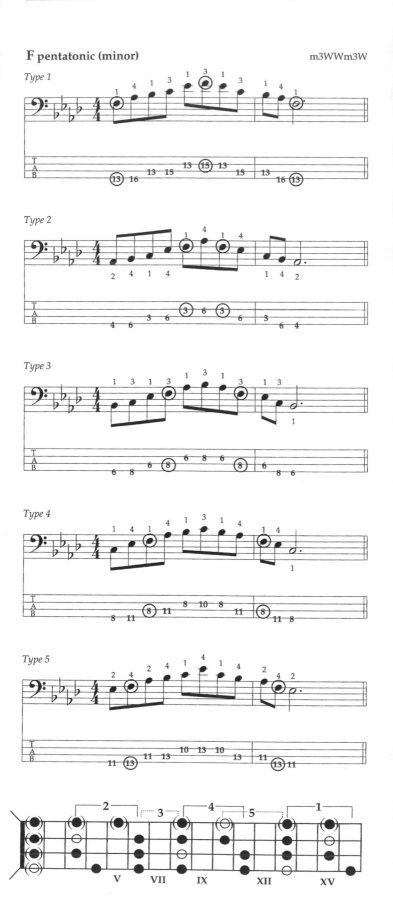

F blues scale (with major third & flatted fifth) m3HHHHm3W

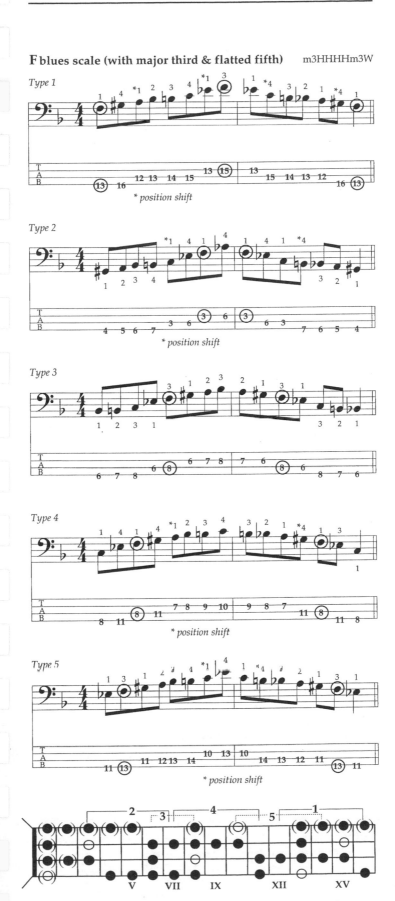

Type 1

* position shift

Type 2

* position shift

Type 3

Type 4

* position shift

Type 5

* position shift

F♯ major (Ionian)

WWHWWWH

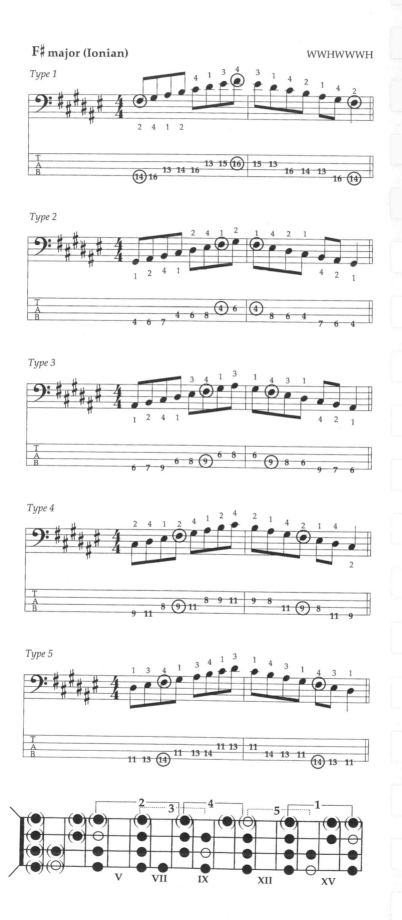

F# natural minor (Aeolian)

WHWWHWW

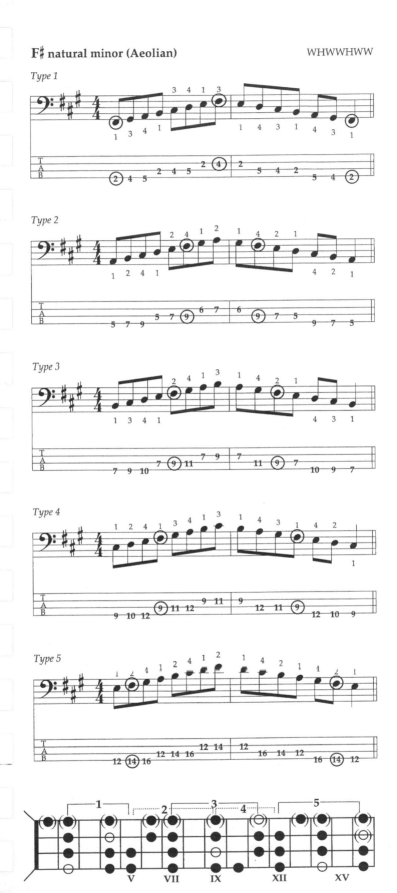

F♯ Dorian

WHWWWHW

Type 1

Type 2

Type 3

Type 4

Type 5

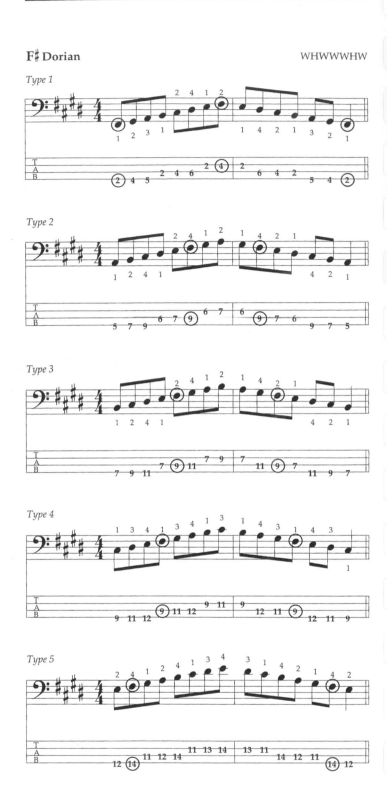

F♯ Phrygian

HWWWHWW

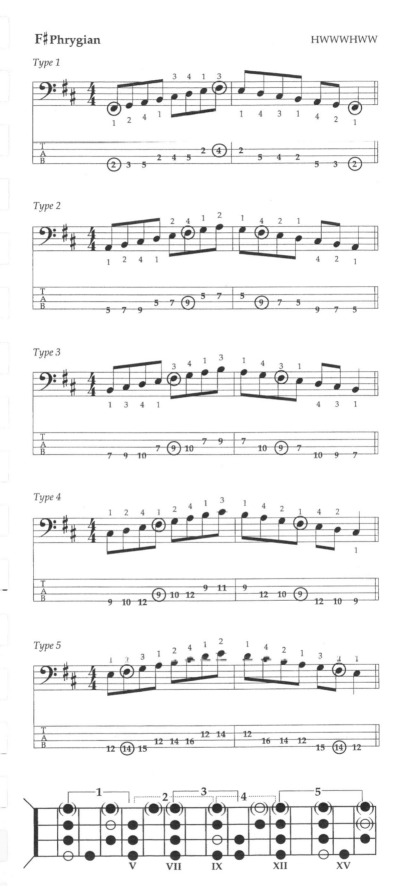

Type 1

Type 2

Type 3

Type 4

Type 5

F#Lydian

WWWHWWH

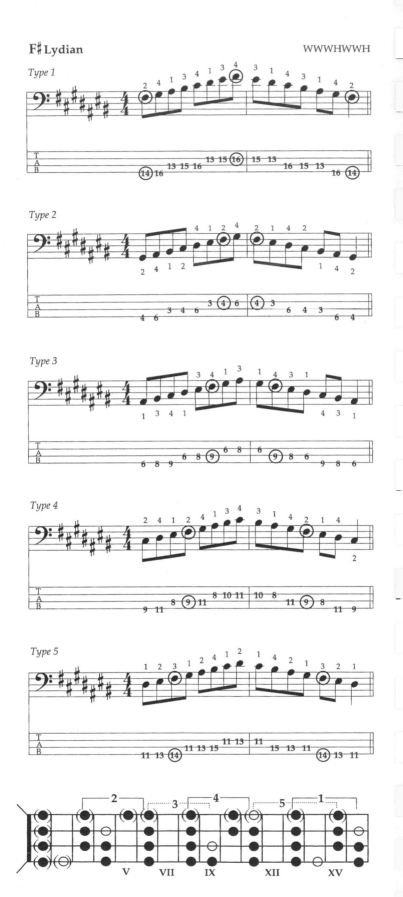

F♯ Mixolydian

WWHWWHW

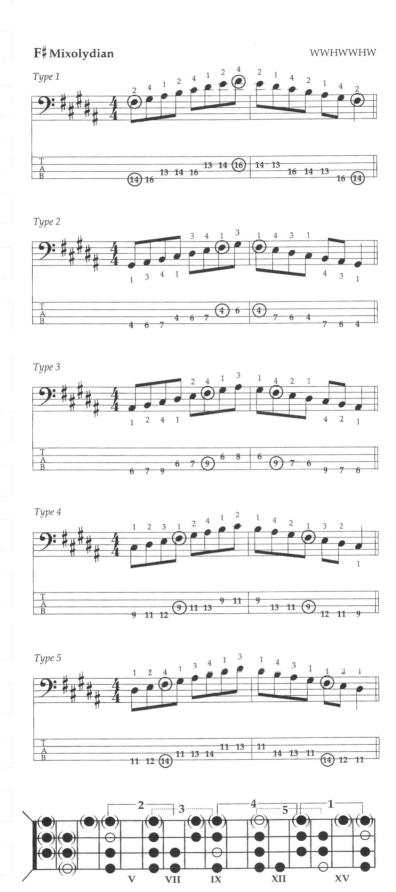

F# Locrian

HWWHWWW

Type 1

Type 2

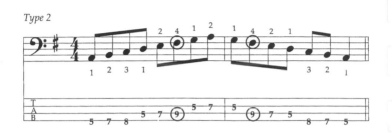

Type 3

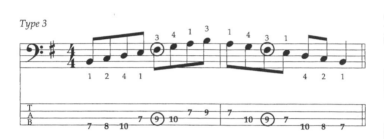

Type 4

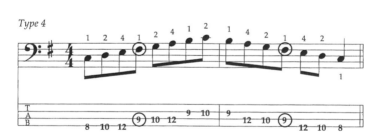

Type 5

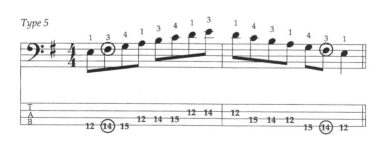

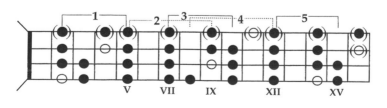

F♯ harmonic minor

WHWWHm3H

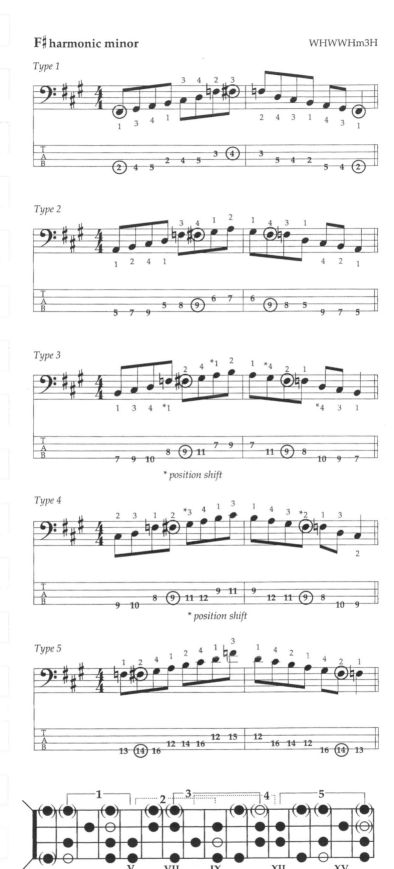

Type 1

Type 2

Type 3

* position shift

Type 4

* position shift

Type 5

F♯ jazz melodic minor

WHWWWWH

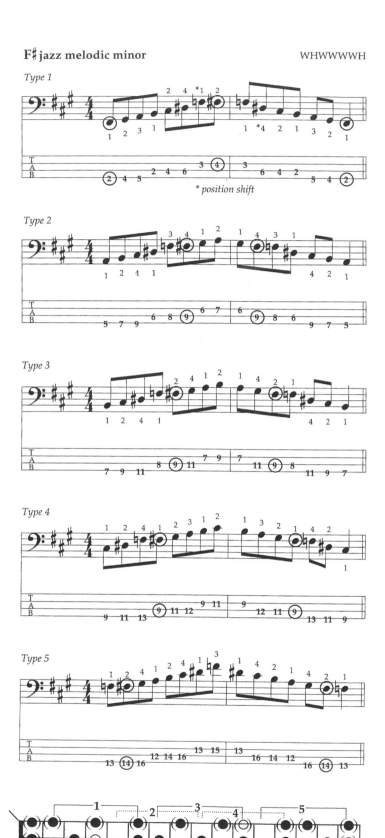

Type 1

* position shift

Type 2

Type 3

Type 4

Type 5

F♯ Lydian flat-seven

WWWHWHW

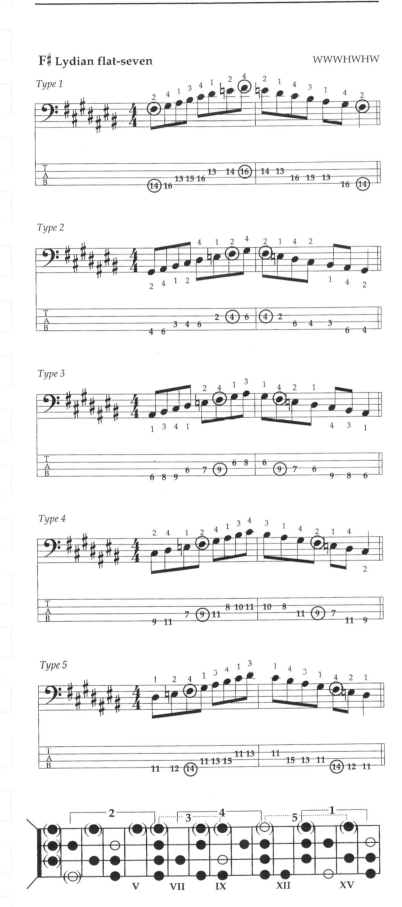

F♯ whole tone

WWWWWW

Type 1

Type 2

F♯ diminished (whole-half)

WHWHWHWH

Type 1

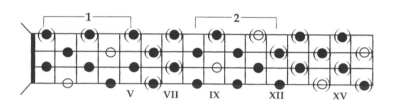

* position shift

Type 2

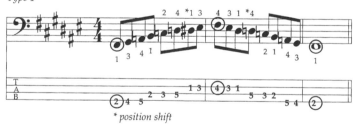

* position shift

F♯ pentatonic (major)

WWm3Wm3

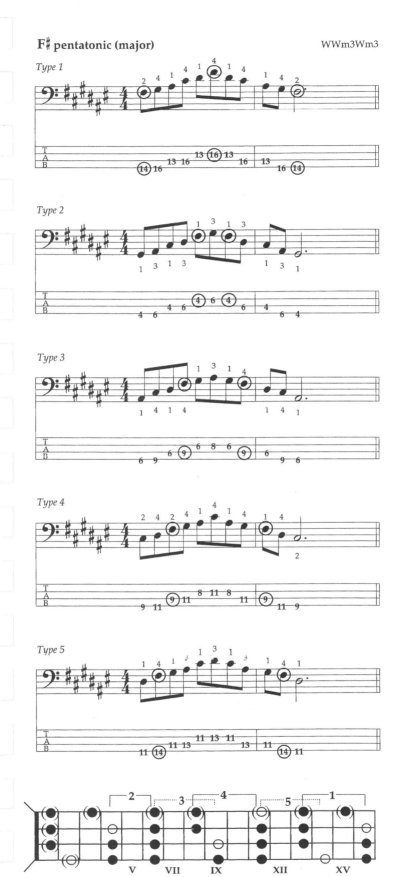

F♯ pentatonic (minor)

m3WWm3W

Type 1

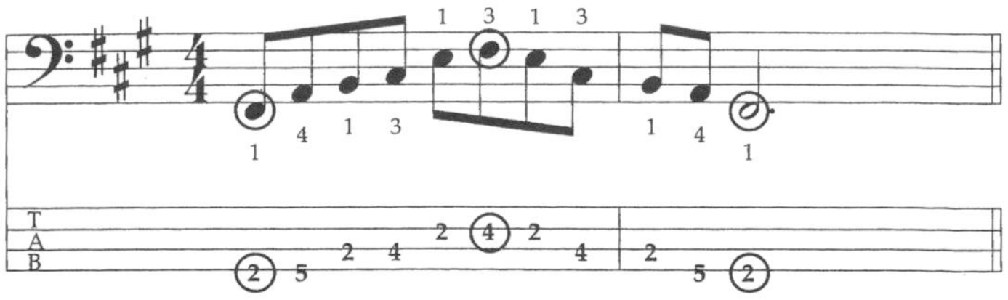

Type 2

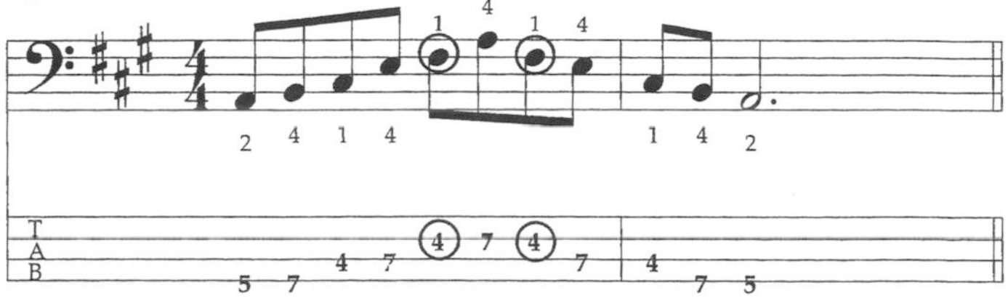

Type 3

Type 4

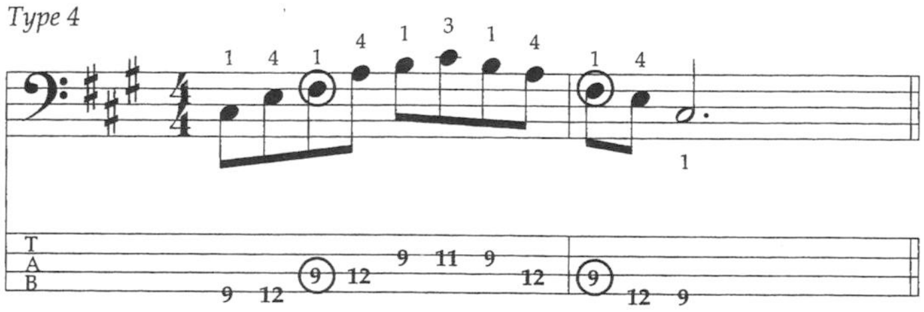

Type 5

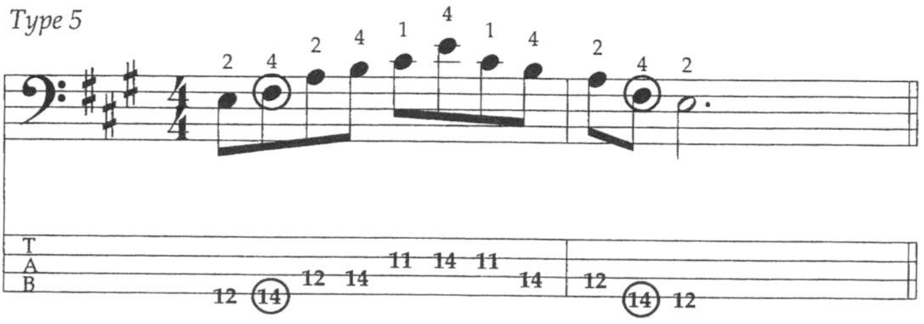

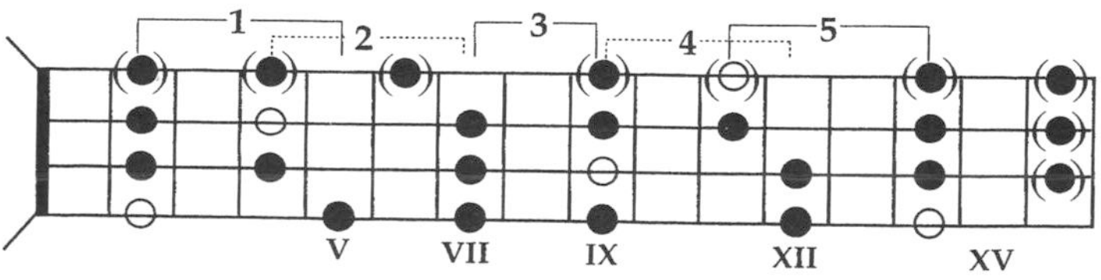

F♯ blues scale (with major third & flatted fifth)   m3HHHHm3W

Type 1

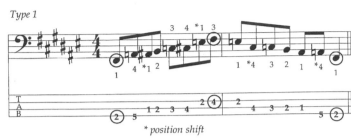

* position shift

Type 2

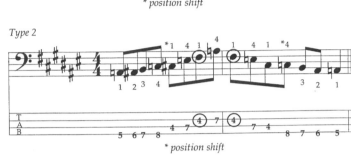

* position shift

Type 3

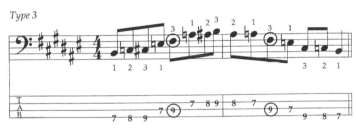

* position shift

Type 4

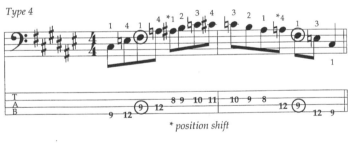

* position shift

Type 5

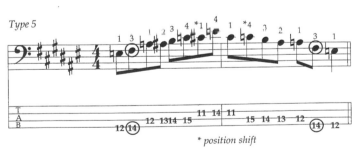

* position shift

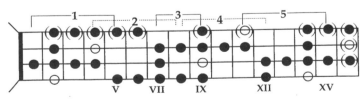

G major (Ionian)

WWHWWWH

Type 1

Type 2

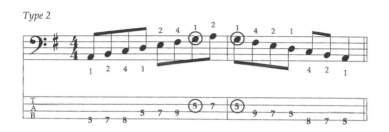

Type 3

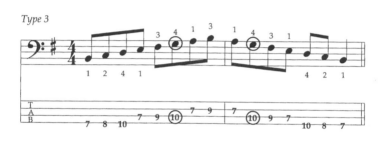

Type 4

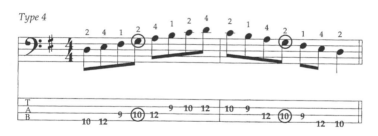

Type 5

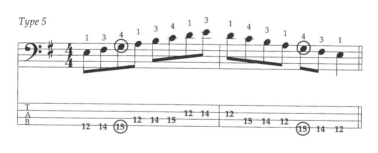

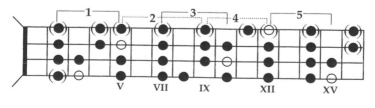

G natural minor (Aeolian)

WHWWHWW

Type 1

Type 2

Type 3

Type 4

Type 5

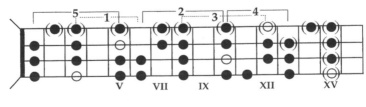

G Dorian

WHWWWHW

Type 1

Type 2

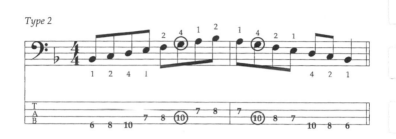

Type 3

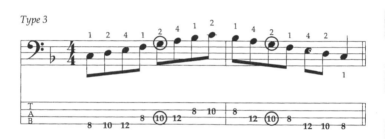

Type 4

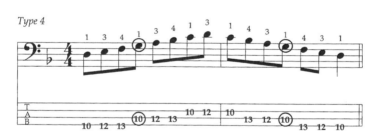

Type 5

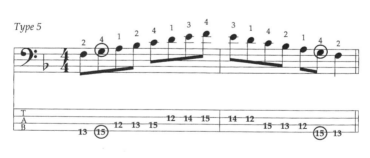

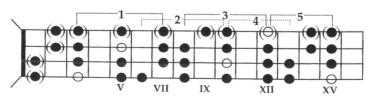

G Phrygian

HWWWHWW

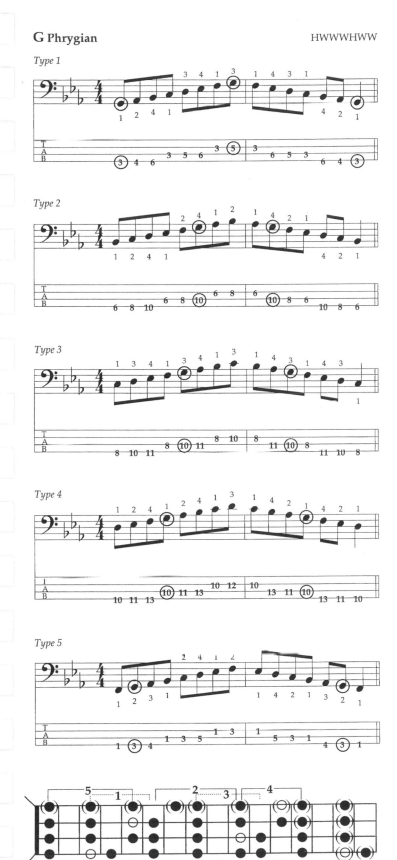

G Lydian

WWWHWWH

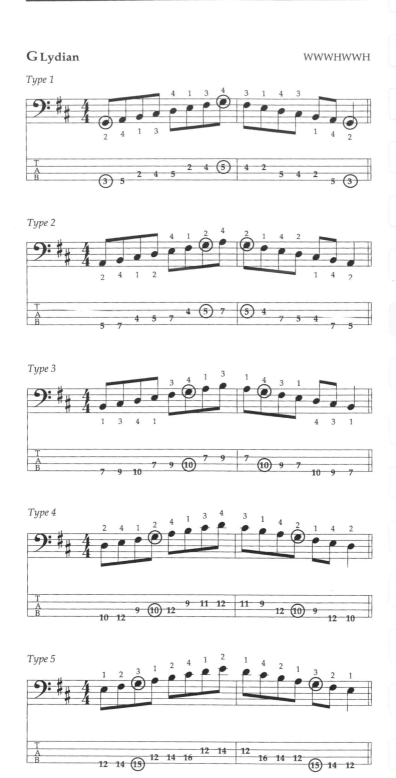

G Mixolydian

WWHWWHW

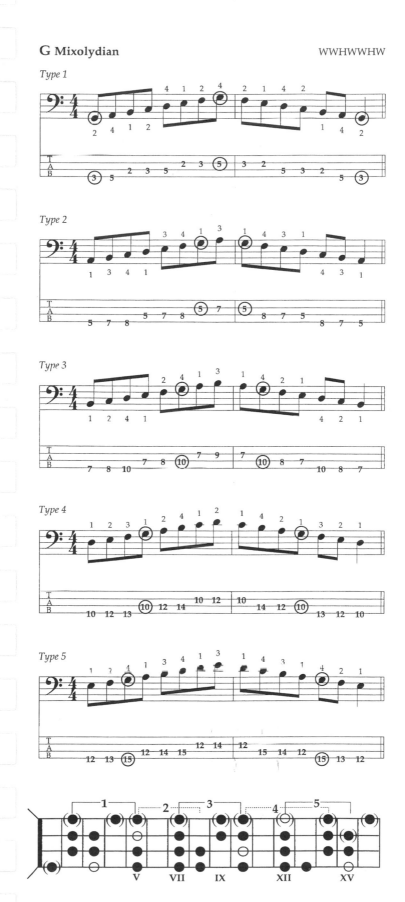

G Locrian

HWWHWWW

Type 1

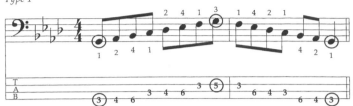

Type 2

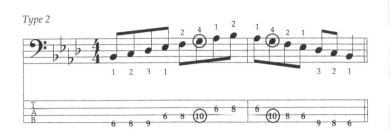

Type 3

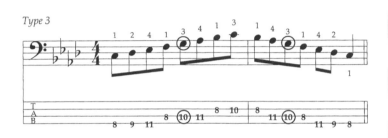

Type 4

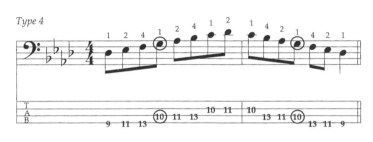

Type 5

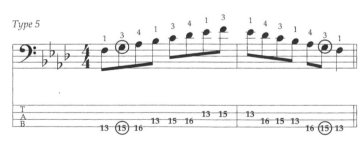

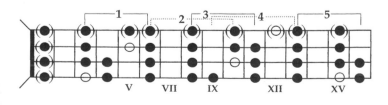

G harmonic minor

WHWWHm3H

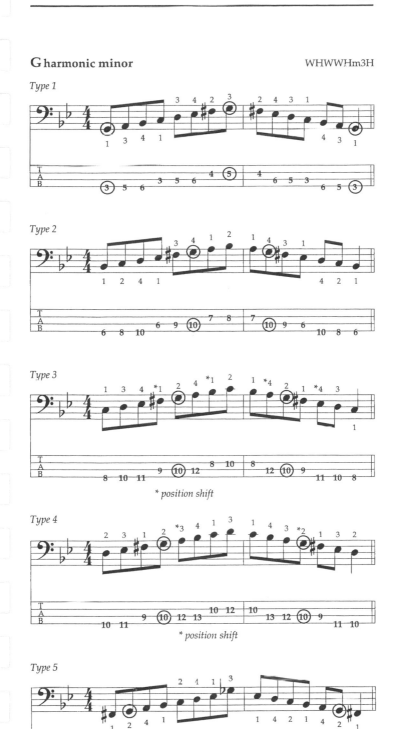

Type 1

Type 2

Type 3

* *position shift*

Type 4

* *position shift*

Type 5

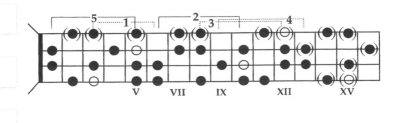

G jazz melodic minor

WHWWWWH

Type 1

* *position shift*

Type 2

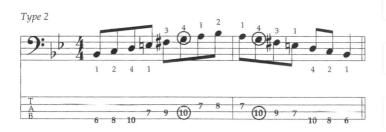

Type 3

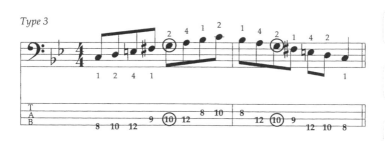

Type 4

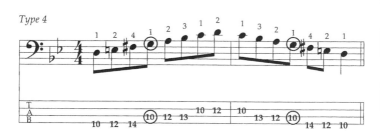

Type 5

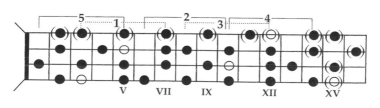

G Lydian flat-seven

WWWHWHW

Type 1

Type 2

Type 3

Type 4

Type 5

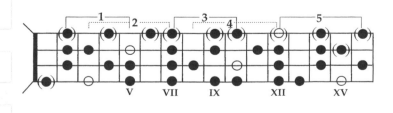

G whole tone

WWWWWW

Type 1

Type 2

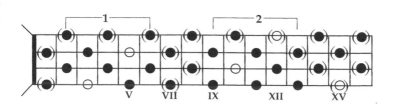

G diminished (whole-half)

WHWHWHWH

Type 1

* position shift

Type 2

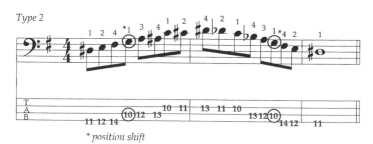

* position shift

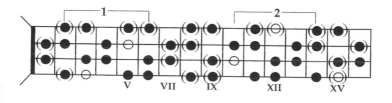

G pentatonic (major)

WWm3Wm3

Type 1

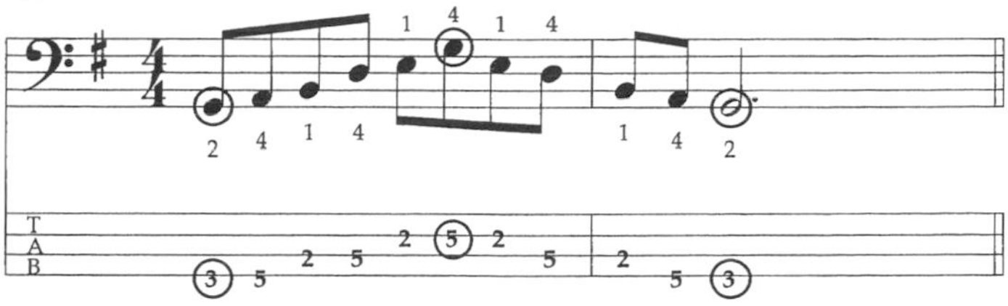

Type 2

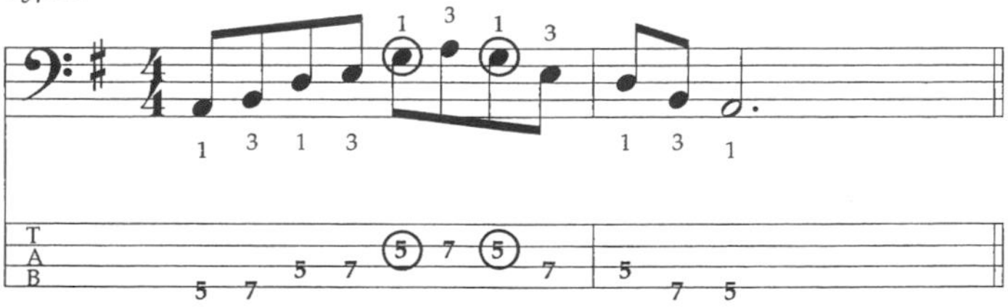

Type 3

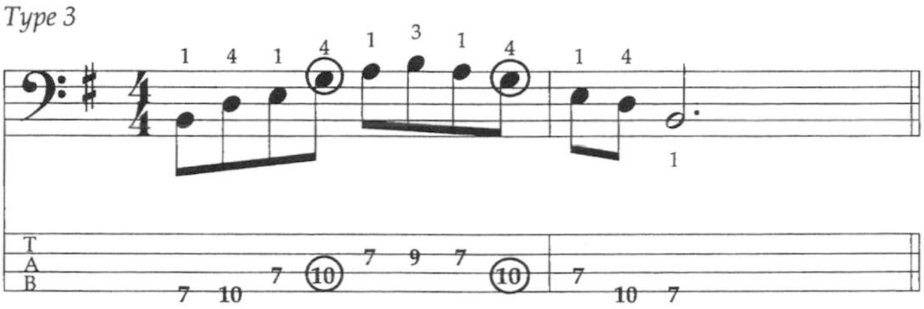

Type 4

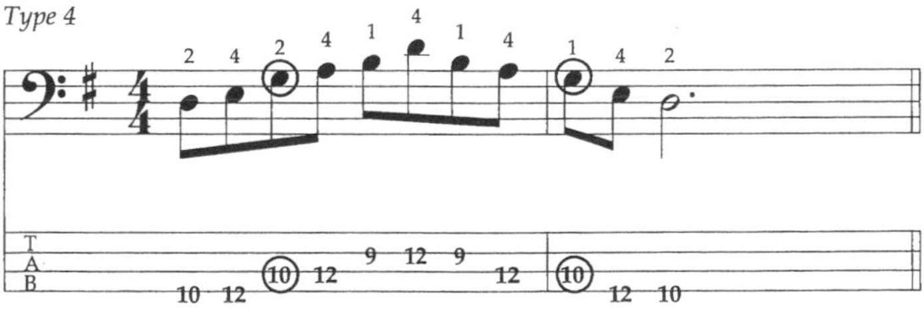

Type 5

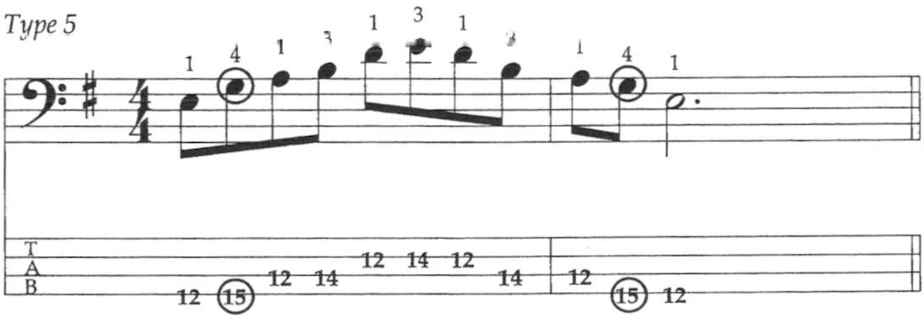

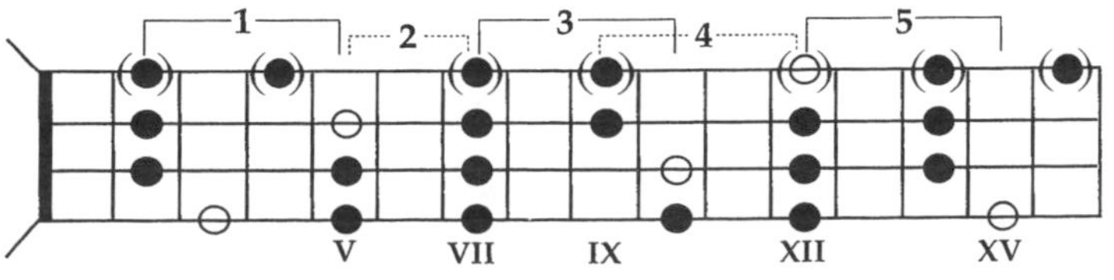

G pentatonic (minor)

m3WWm3W

Type 1

Type 2

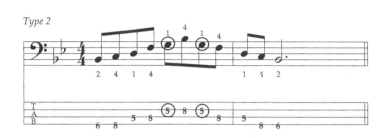

Type 3

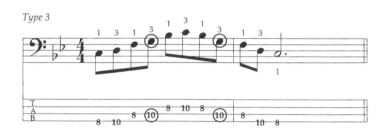

Type 4

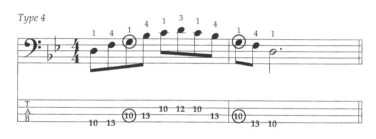

Type 5

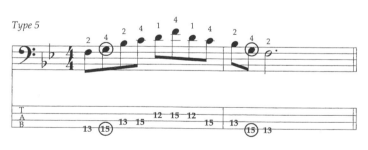

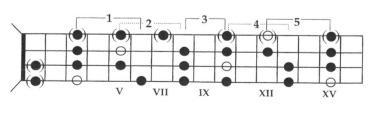

G blues scale (with major third & flatted fifth) m3HHHHm3W

Type 1

* position shift

Type 2

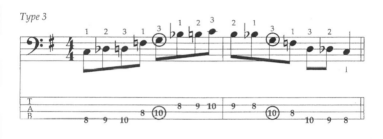

* position shift

Type 3

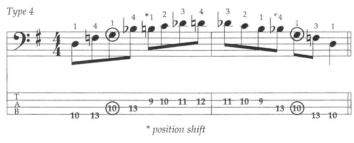

Type 4

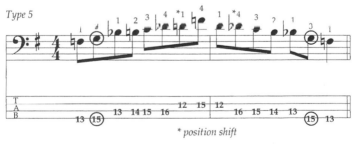

* position shift

Type 5

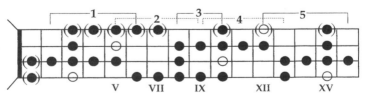

* position shift

A♭ major (Ionian)

WWHWWWH

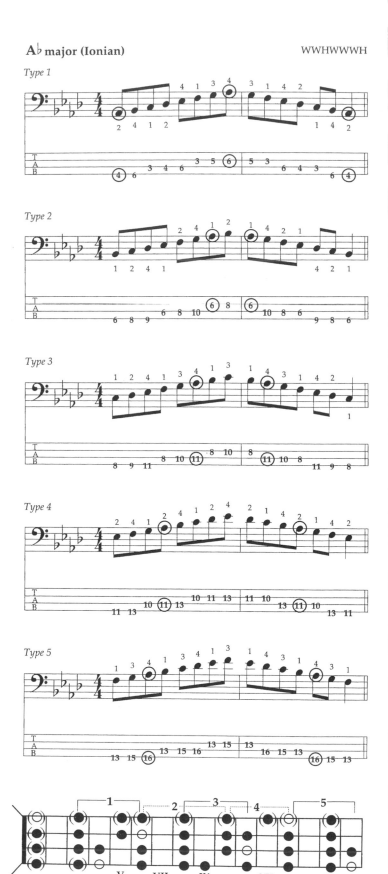

A♭ natural minor (Aeolian)

WHWWHWW

Type 1

Type 2

Type 3

Type 4

Type 5

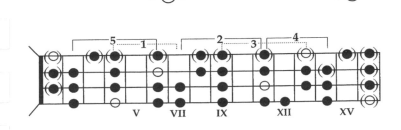

A♭ Dorian

WHWWWHW

G#/Ab Phrygian

HWWWHWW

Type 1

Type 2

Type 3

Type 4

Type 5

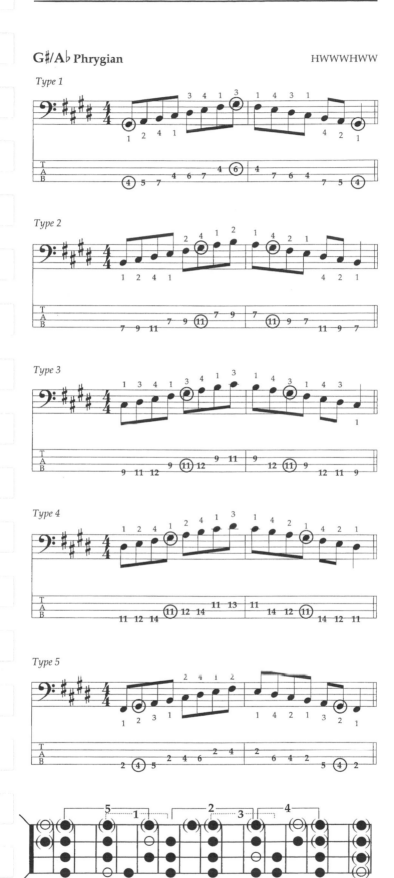

A♭ Lydian

WWWHWWH

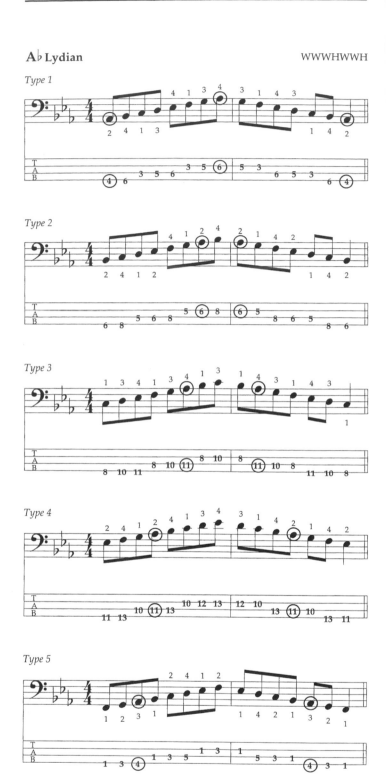

Type 1

Type 2

Type 3

Type 4

Type 5

A♭ Mixolydian

WWHWWHW

G♯/A♭ Locrian

HWWHWWW

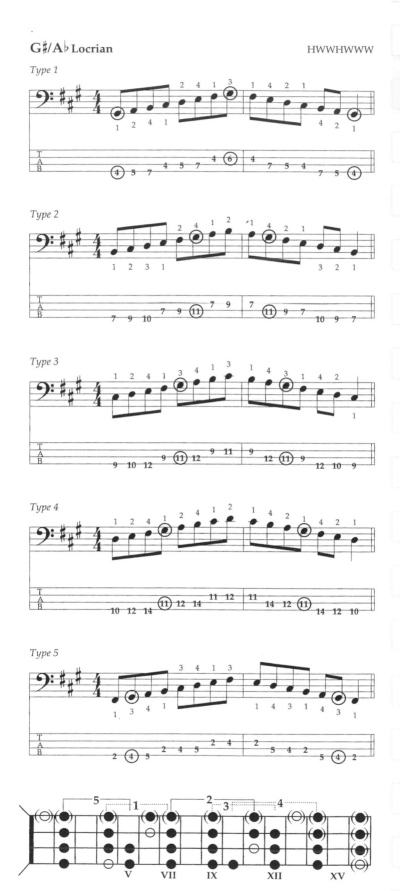

A♭ harmonic minor

WHWWHm3H

Type 1

Type 2

Type 3

* *position shift*

Type 4

* *position shift*

Type 5

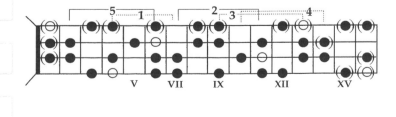

A♭ jazz melodic minor

WHWWWWH

Type 1

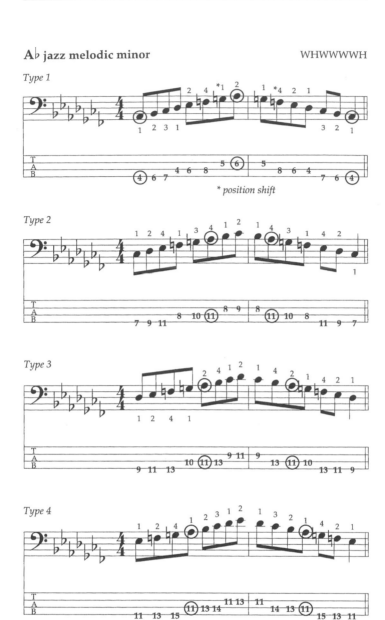

* position shift

Type 2

Type 3

Type 4

Type 5

A♭ Lydian flat-seven

WWWHWHW

Type 1

Type 2

Type 3

Type 4

Type 5

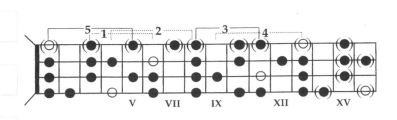

A♭ whole tone

WWWWWW

Type 1

Type 2

A♭ diminished (whole-half)

WHWHWHWH

Type 1

* position shift

Type 2

* position shift

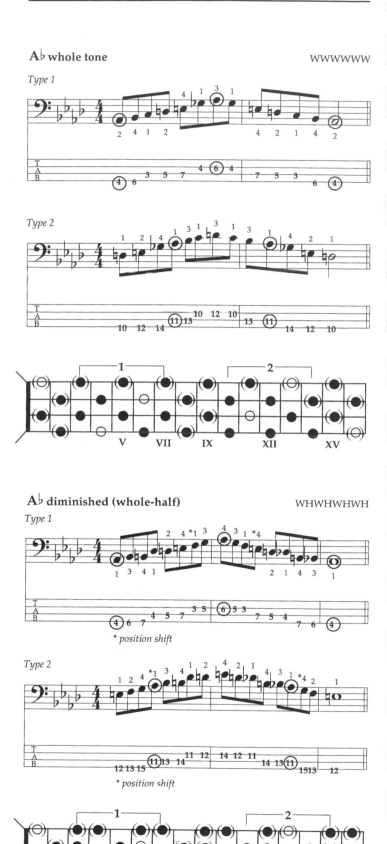

A♭ pentatonic (major)

WWm3Wm3

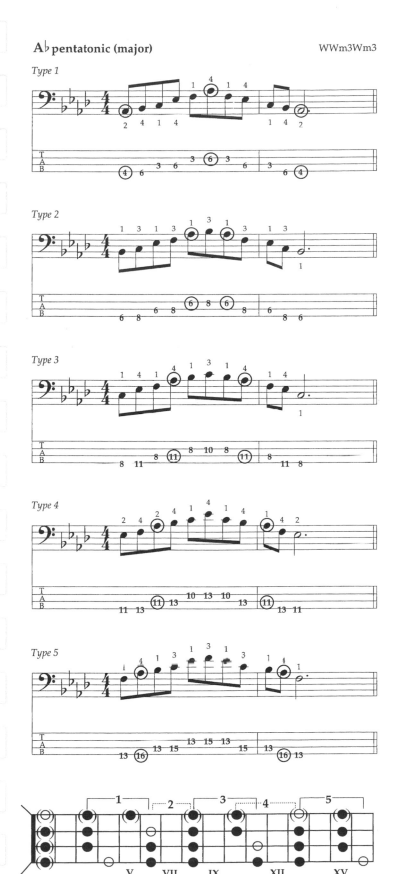

A♭ pentatonic (minor)

m3WWm3W

Type 1

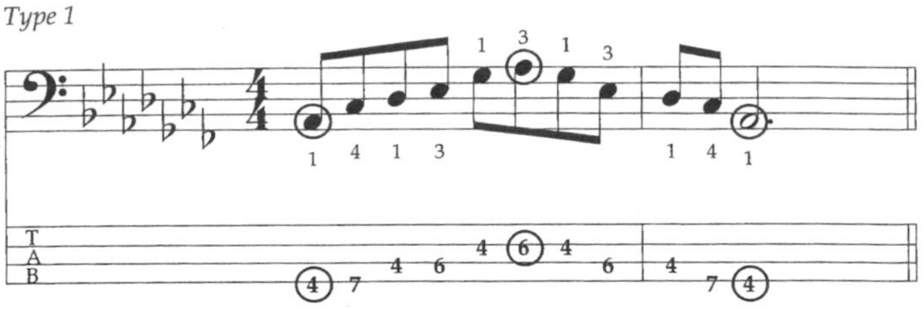

Type 2

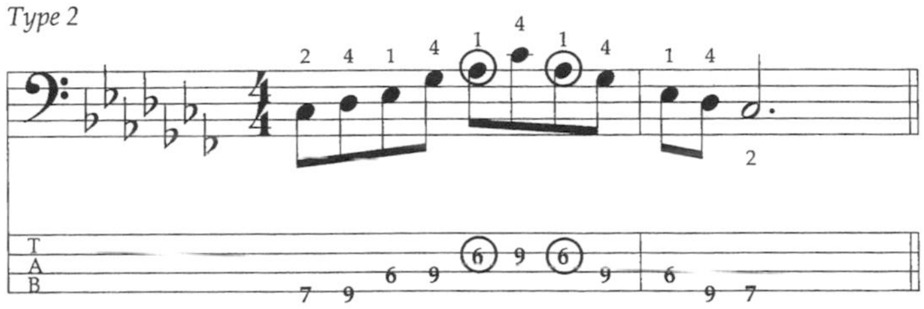

Type 3

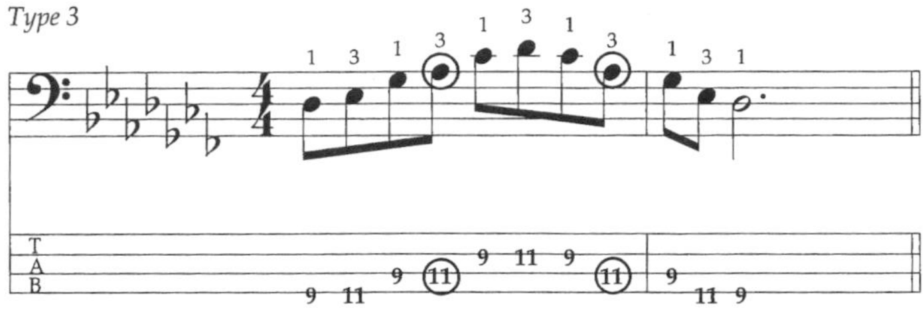

Type 4

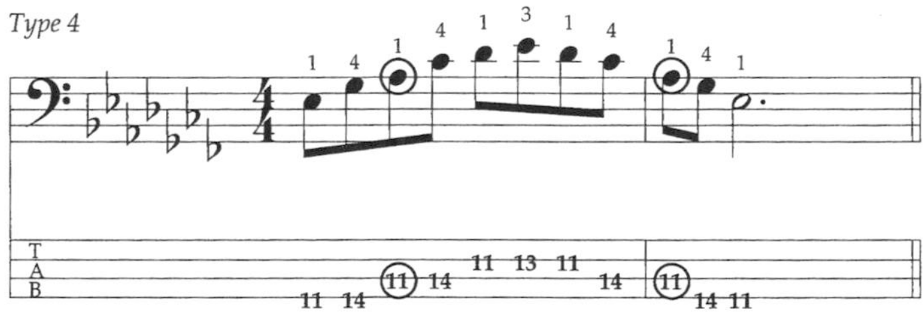

Type 5

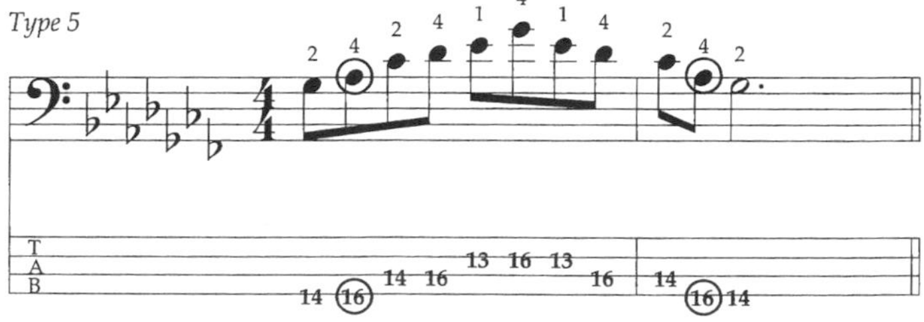

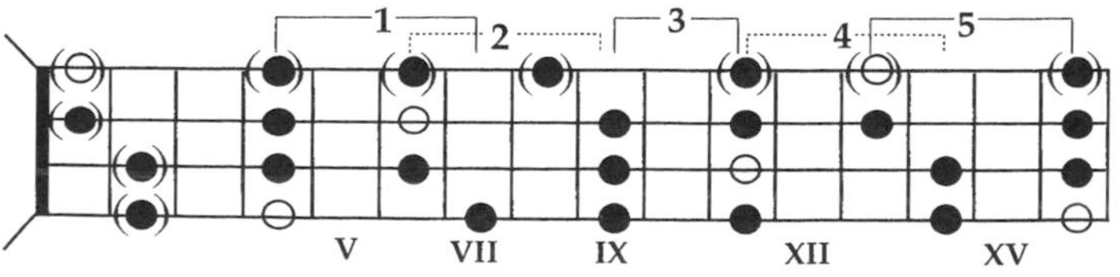

A♭ blues scale (with major third & flatted fifth) m3HHHHm3W

Type 1

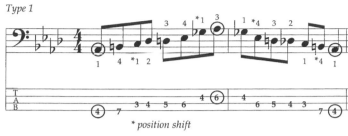

* *position shift*

Type 2

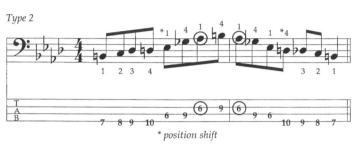

* *position shift*

Type 3

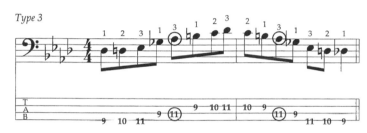

Type 4

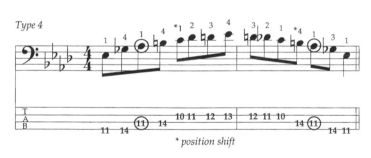

* *position shift*

Type 5

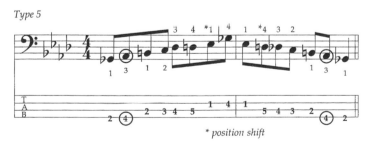

* *position shift*

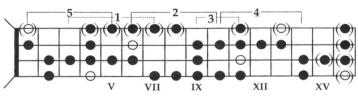

A major (Ionian)

WWHWWWH

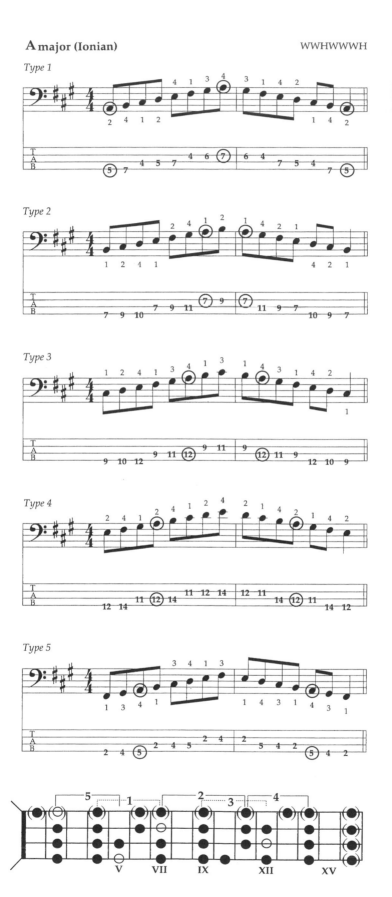

Type 1

Type 2

Type 3

Type 4

Type 5

A natural minor (Aeolian)

WHWWHWW

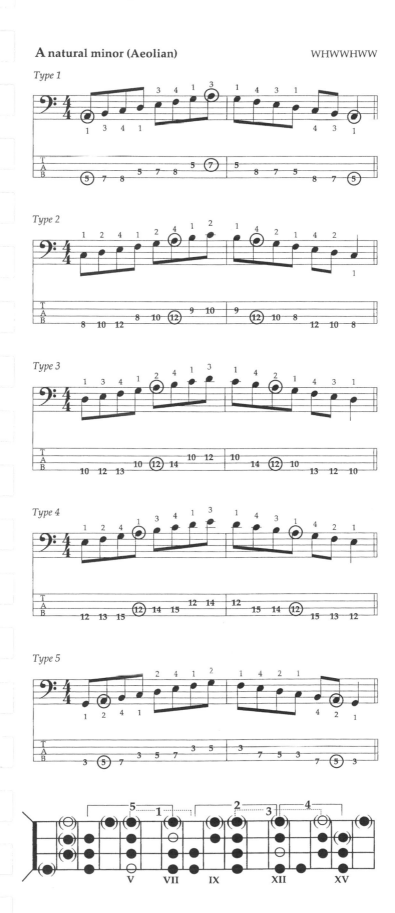

A Dorian

WHWWWHW

Type 1

Type 2

Type 3

Type 4

Type 5

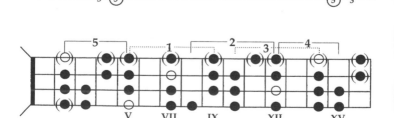

A Phrygian

HWWWHWW

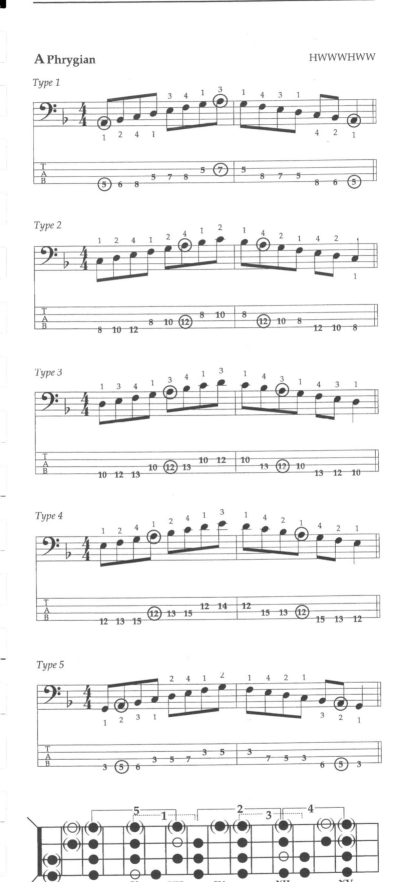

A Lydian

WWWHWWH

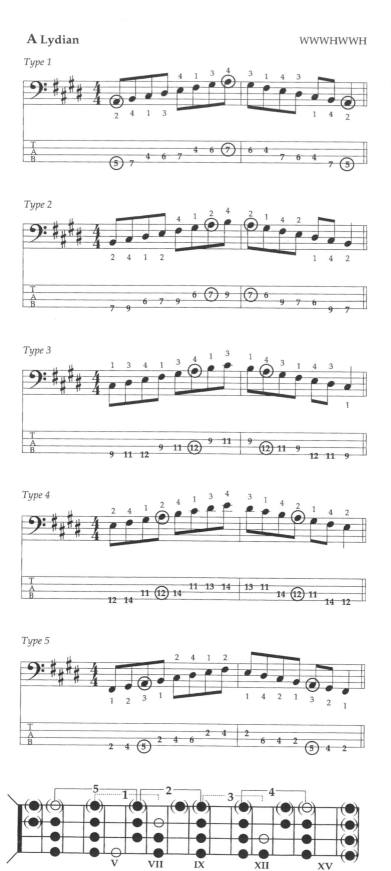

A Mixolydian

WWHWWHW

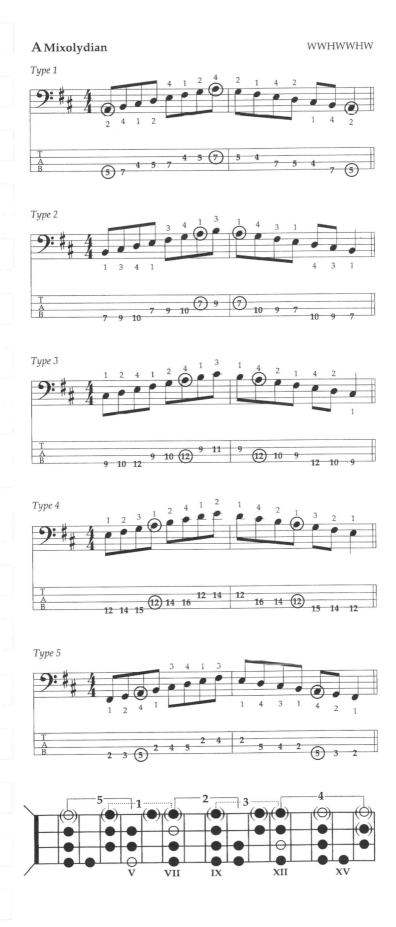

A Locrian

HWWHWWW

Type 1

Type 2

Type 3

Type 4

Type 5

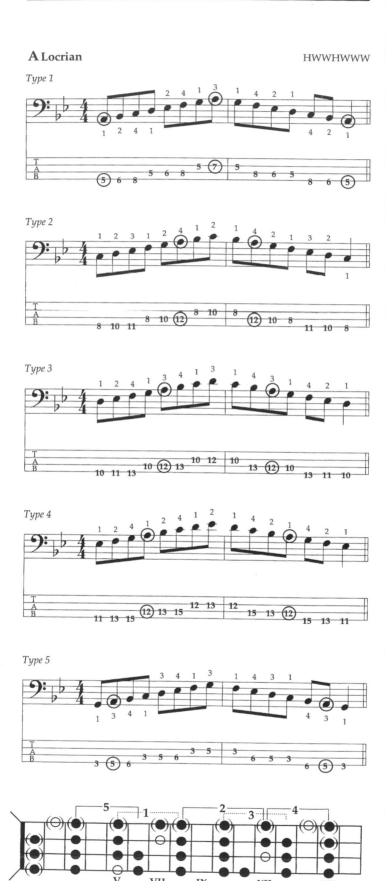

A harmonic minor

WHWWHm3H

Type 1

Type 2

Type 3

*position shift

Type 4

*position shift

Type 5

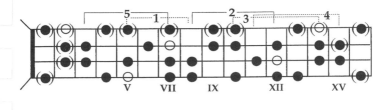

A jazz melodic minor

WHWWWWH

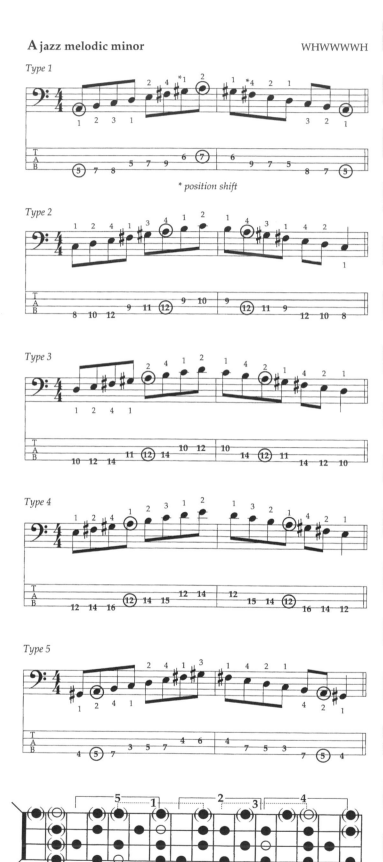

Type 1

* position shift

Type 2

Type 3

Type 4

Type 5

A Lydian flat-seven

WWWHWHW

Type 1

Type 2

Type 3

Type 4

Type 5

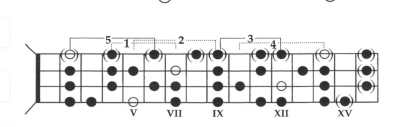

A whole tone

WWWWWW

Type 1

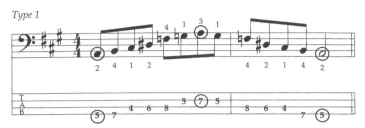

Type 2

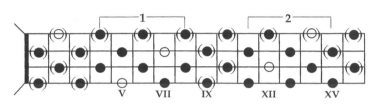

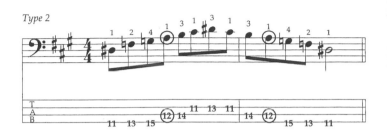

A diminished (whole-half)

WHWHWHWH

Type 1

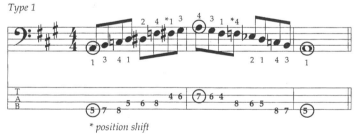

position shift

Type 2

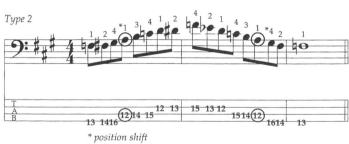

position shift

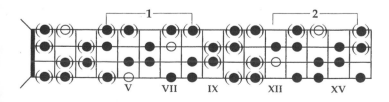

A pentatonic (major)

WWm3Wm3

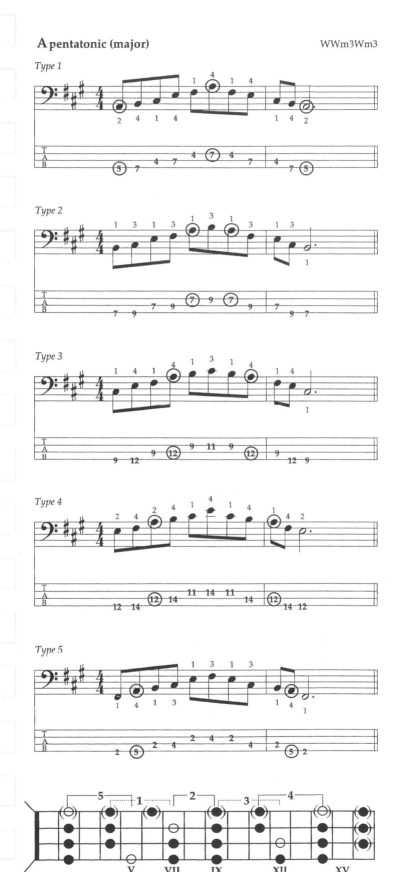

A pentatonic (minor)

m3WWm3W

Type 1

Type 2

Type 3

Type 4

Type 5

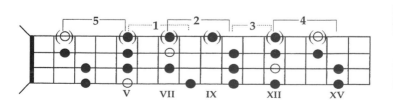

A blues scale (with major third & flatted fifth)   m3HHHHm3W

Type 1

* position shift

Type 2

* position shift

Type 3

Type 4

* position shift

Type 5

* position shift

B♭ major (Ionian)

WWHWWWH

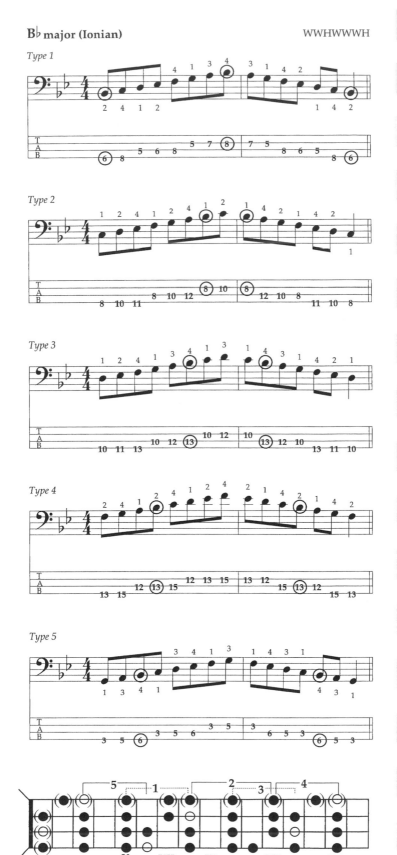

B♭ natural minor (Aeolian)

WHWWHWW

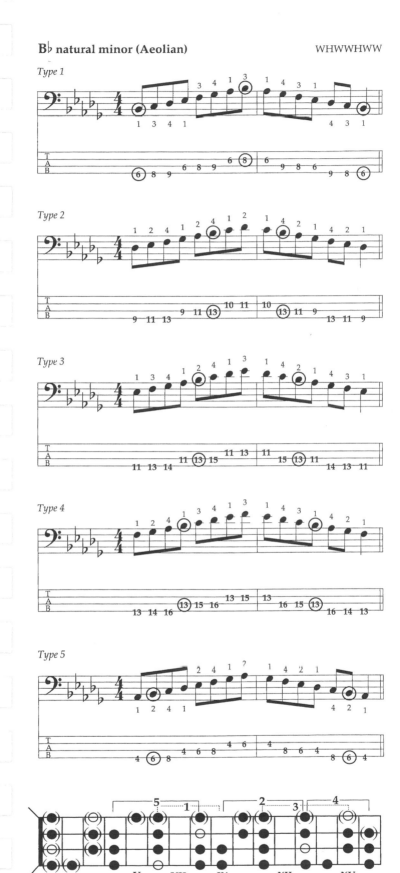

B♭ Dorian

WHWWWHW

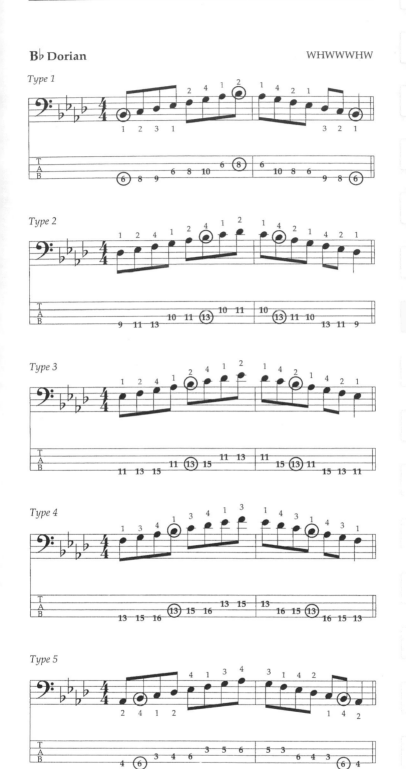

B♭ Phrygian

HWWWHWW

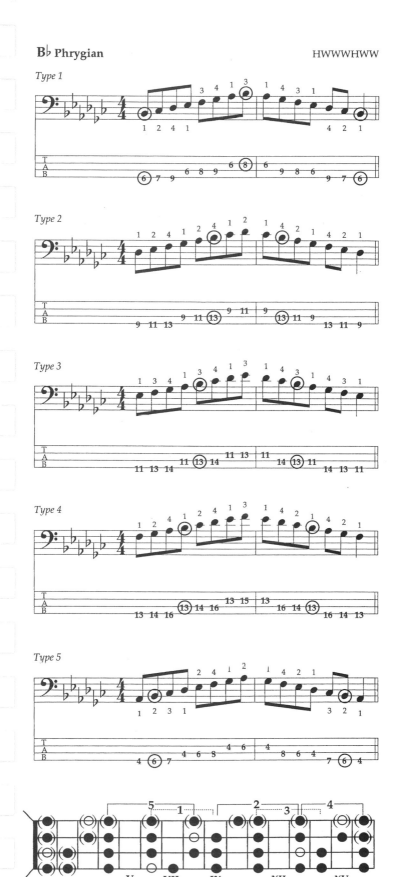

B♭ Lydian

WWWHWWH

Type 1

Type 2

Type 3

Type 4

Type 5

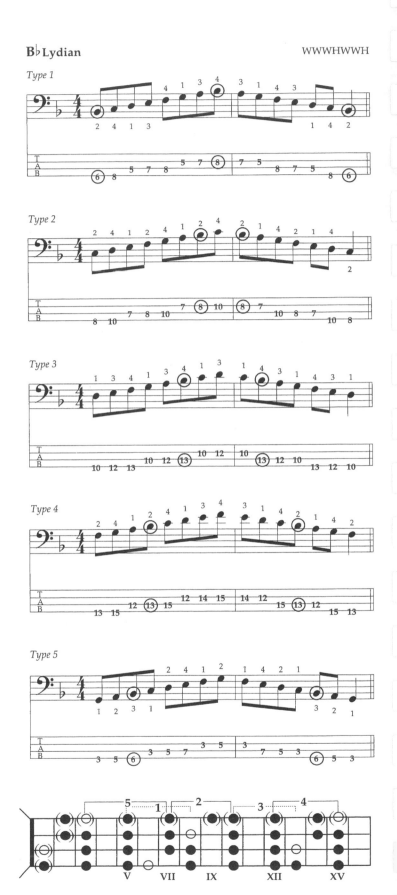

B♭ Mixolydian

WWHWWHW

Type 1

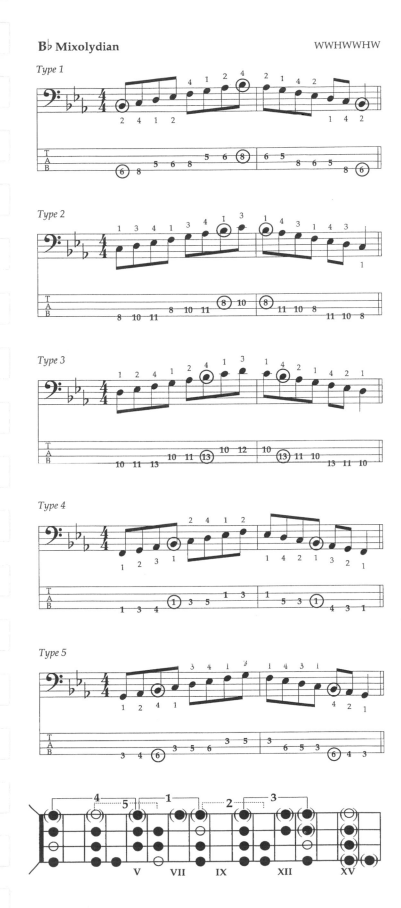

Type 2

Type 3

Type 4

Type 5

B♭ Locrian

HWWHWWW

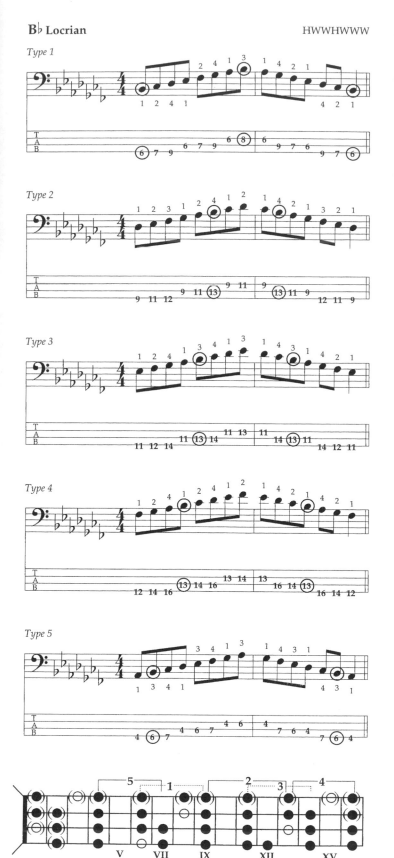

B♭ harmonic minor

WHWWHm3H

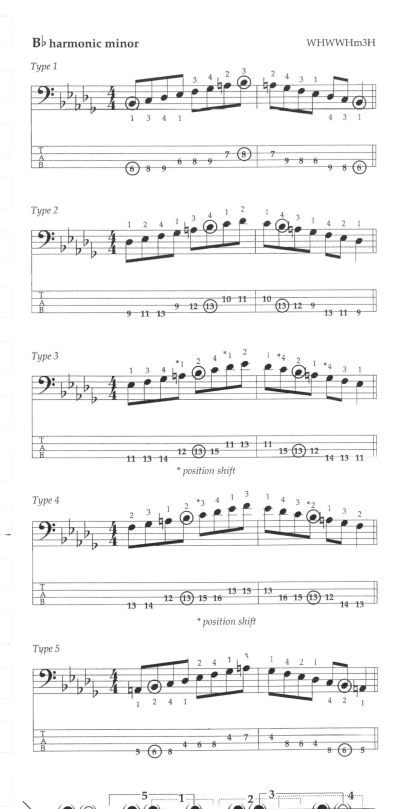

Type 1

Type 2

Type 3

* position shift

Type 4

* position shift

Type 5

B♭ jazz melodic minor

WHWWWWH

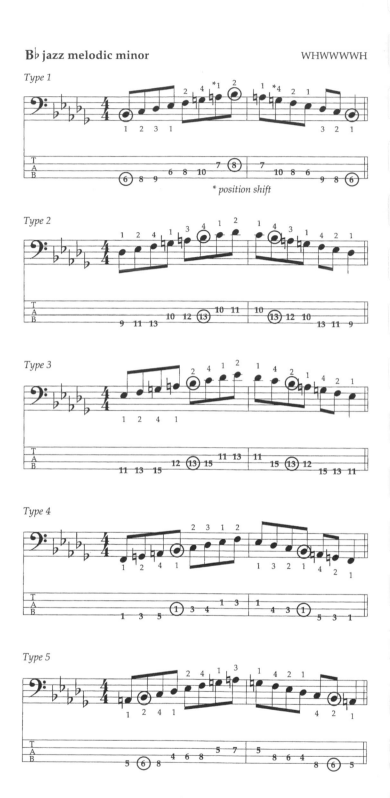

Type 1

position shift

Type 2

Type 3

Type 4

Type 5

B♭ Lydian flat-seven

WWWHWHW

Type 1

Type 2

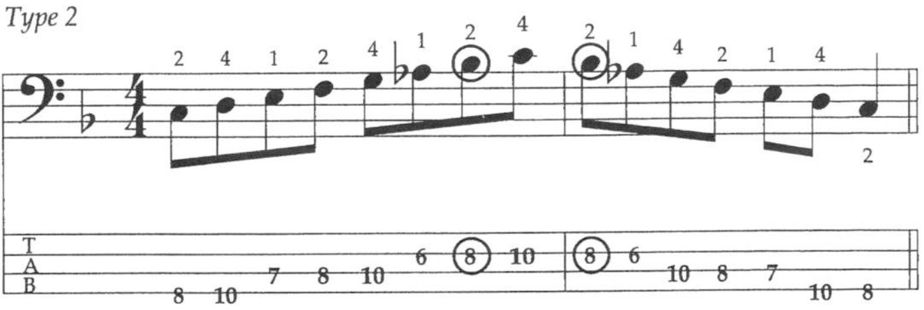

Type 3

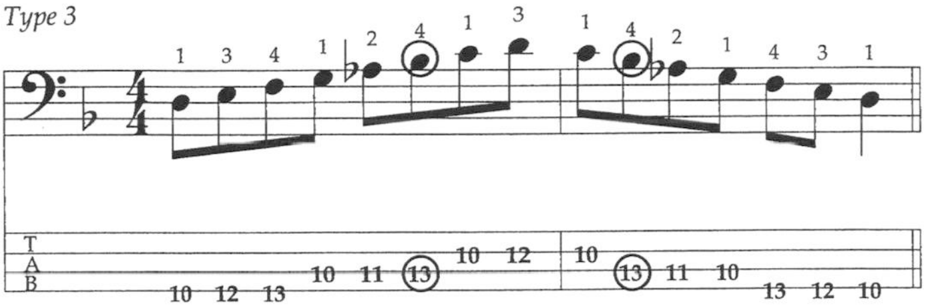

Type 4

Type 5

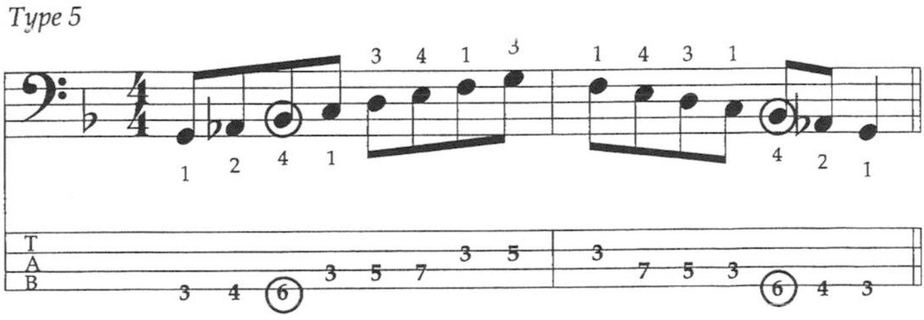

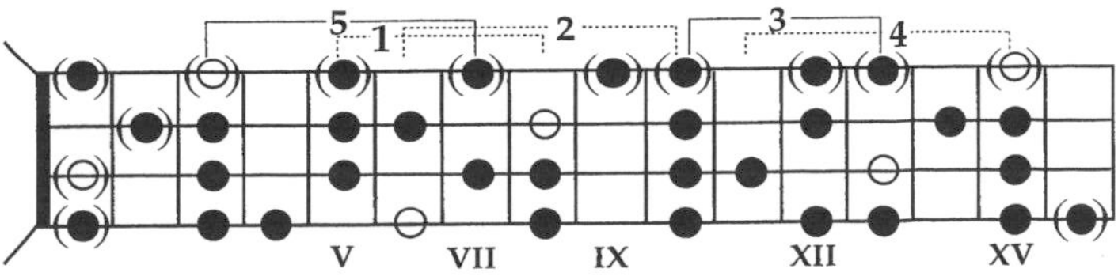

B♭ whole tone

WWWWWW

Type 1

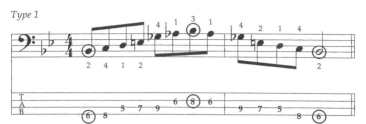

Type 2

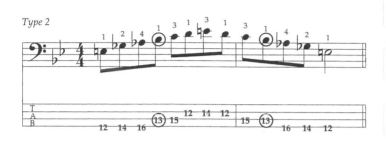

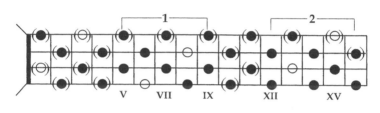

B♭ diminished (whole-half)

WHWHWHWH

Type 1

position shift

Type 2

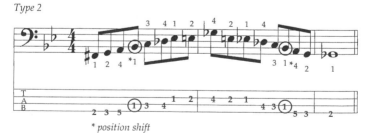

position shift

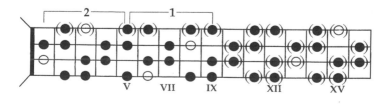

B♭ pentatonic (major)

WWm3Wm3

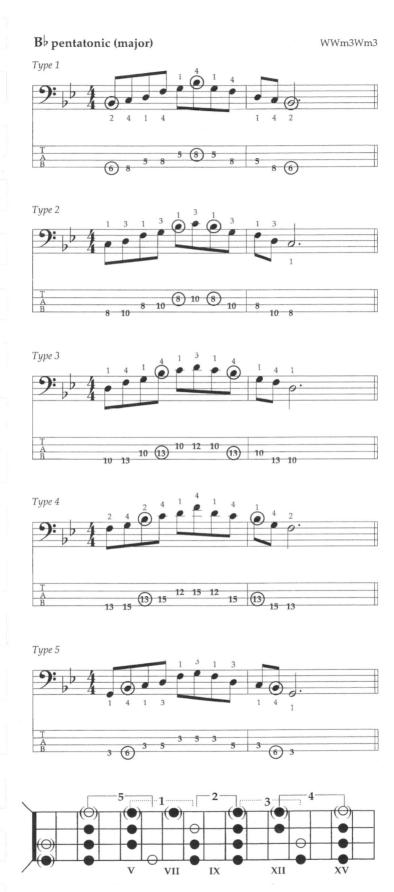

B♭ pentatonic (minor)

m3WWm3W

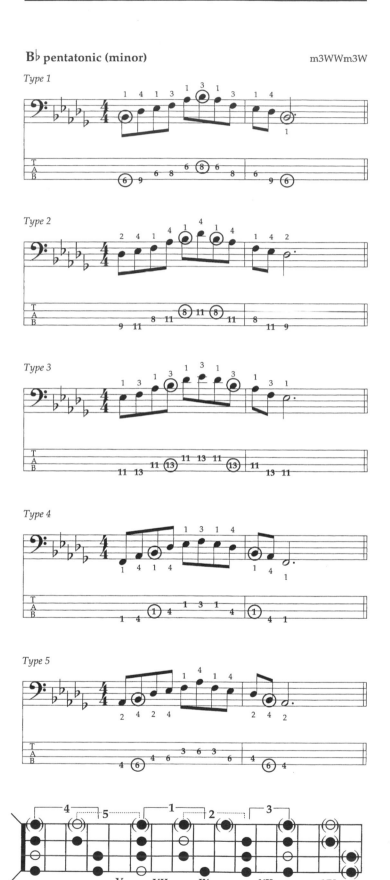

B♭ blues scale (with major third & flatted fifth)   m3HHHHm3W

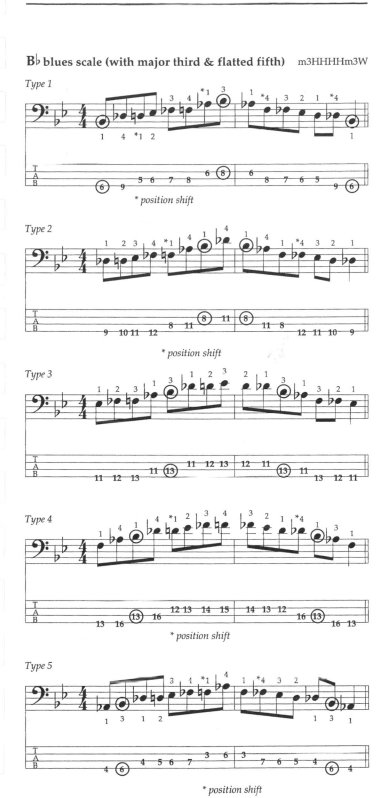

B major (Ionian)

WWHWWWH

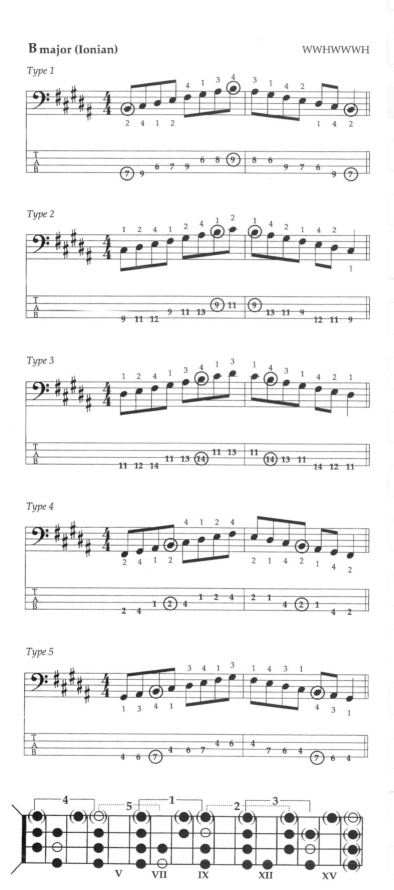

Type 1

Type 2

Type 3

Type 4

Type 5

B natural minor (Aeolian)

WHWWHWW

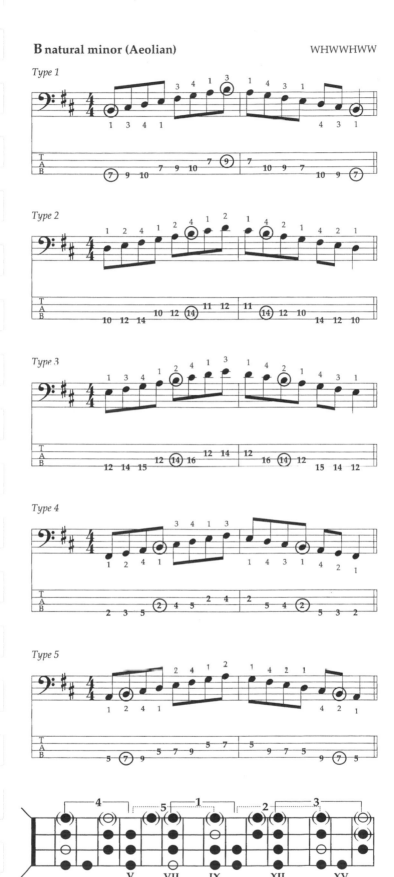

B Dorian

WHWWWHW

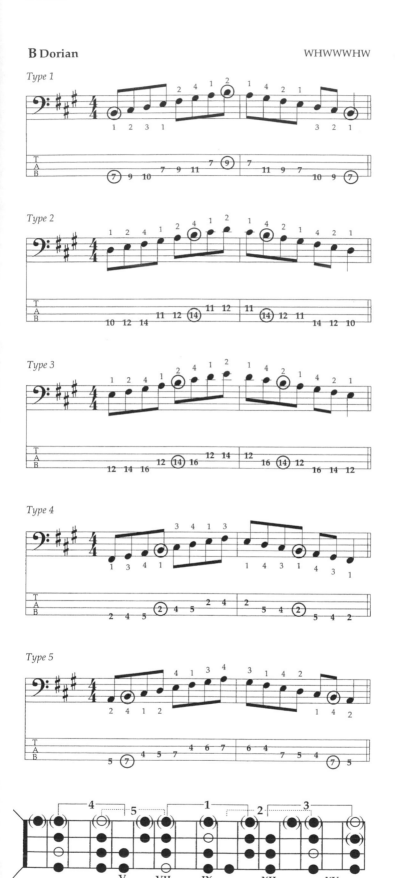

B Phrygian

HWWWHWW

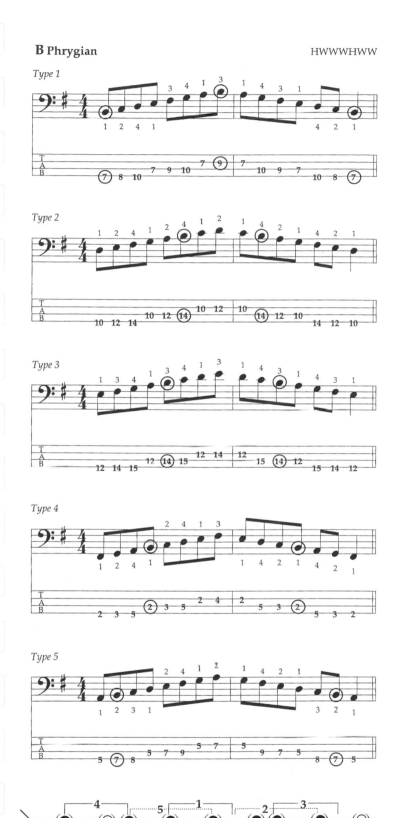

Type 1

Type 2

Type 3

Type 4

Type 5

B Lydian

WWWHWWH

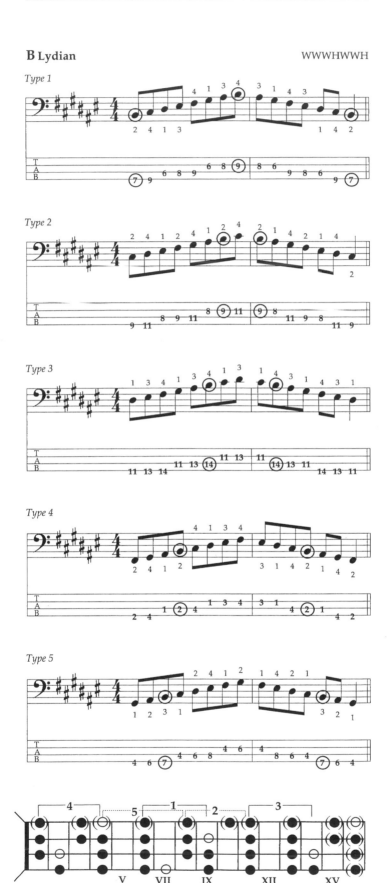

B Mixolydian

WWHWWHW

Type 1

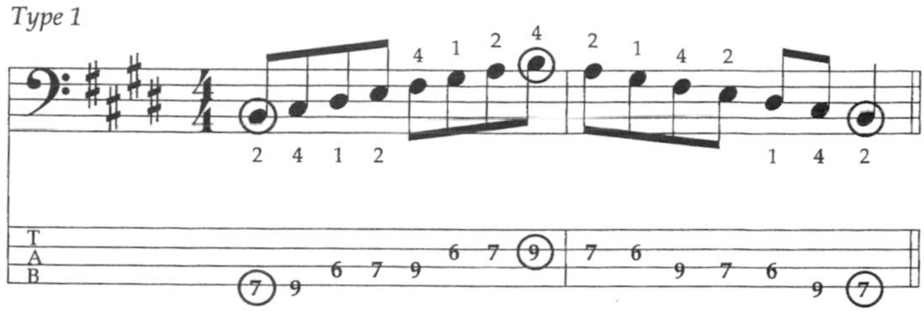

Type 2

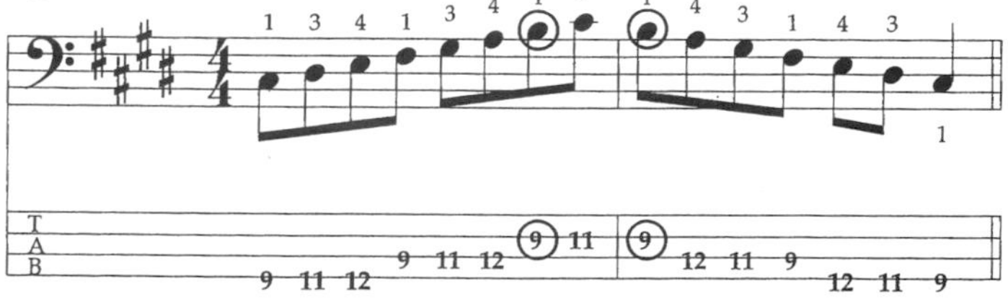

Type 3

Type 4

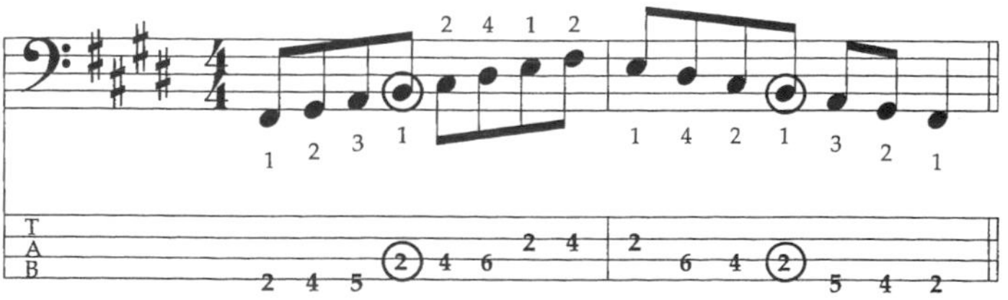

Type 5

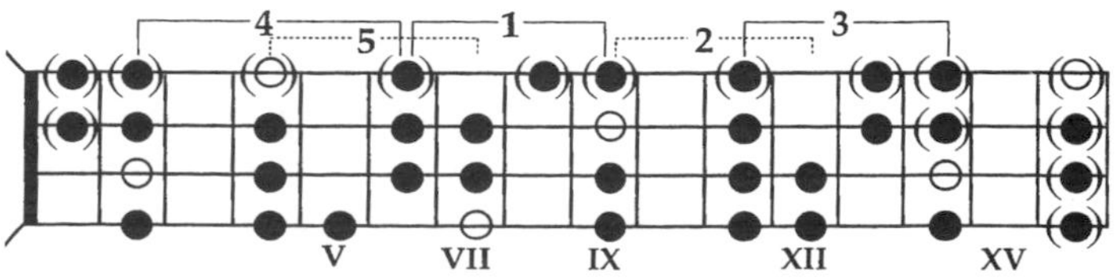

B Locrian

HWWHWWW

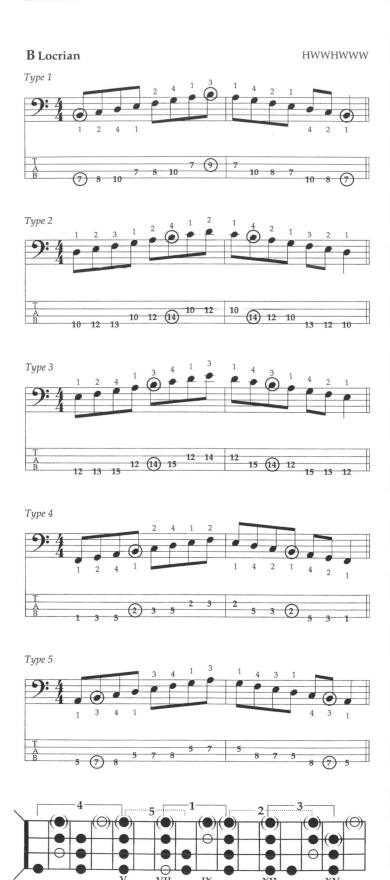

B harmonic minor

WHWWHm3H

Type 1

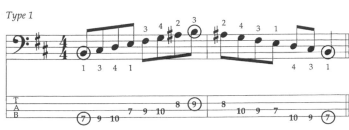

Type 2

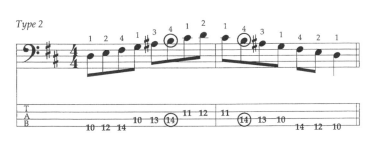

Type 3

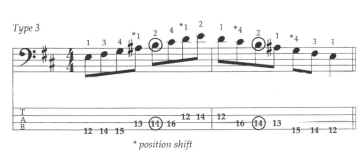

* position shift

Type 4

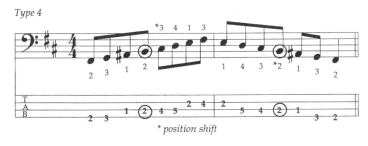

* position shift

Type 5

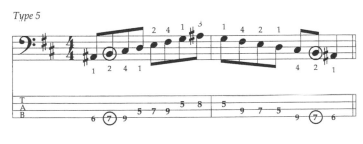

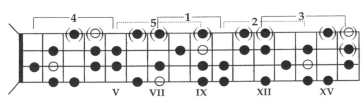

B jazz melodic minor

WHWWWWH

Type 1

* position shift

Type 2

Type 3

Type 4

Type 5

B Lydian flat-seven

WWWHWHW

Type 1

Type 2

Type 3

Type 4

Type 5

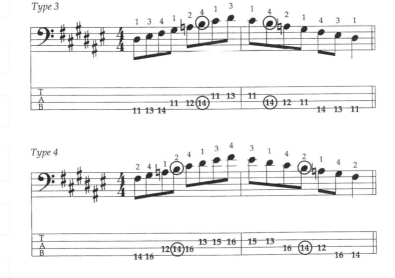

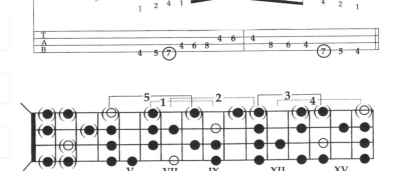

B whole tone

WWWWWW

Type 1

Type 2

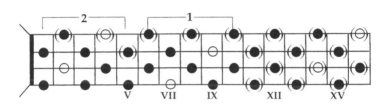

B diminished (whole-half)

WHWHWHWH

Type 1

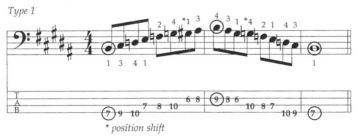

Type 2

* position shift

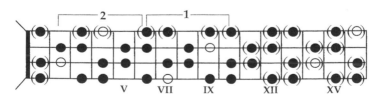

B pentatonic (major)

WWm3Wm3

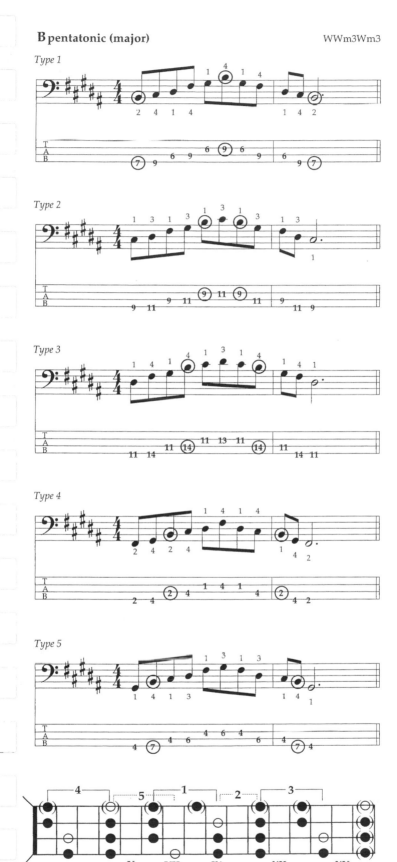

B pentatonic (minor)

m3WWm3W

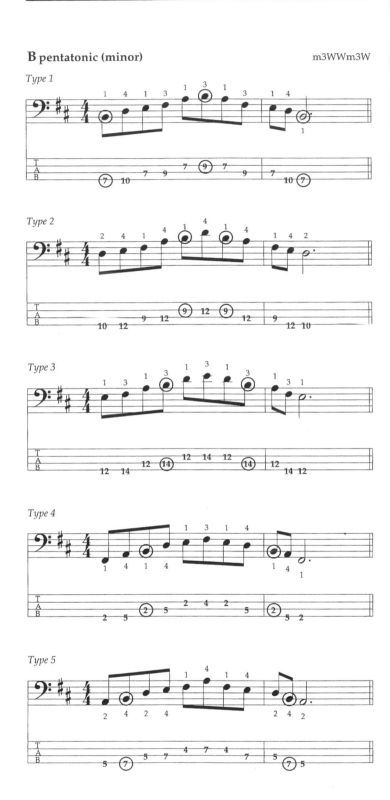

B blues scale (with major third & flatted fifth)   m3HHHHm3W

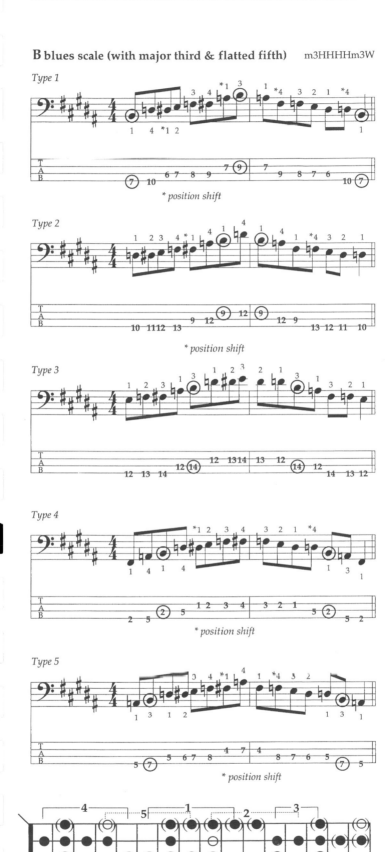